AQA Accounting

Exclusively endorsed by AQA

A2

Yong Situ.

Jake Dabson

Claire Merrills

Jacqueline Halls-Bryan

Nelson Thornes

Text © Claire Merrills, Jacqueline Halls-Bryan 2009
Original illustrations © Nelson Thornes Ltd 2009

Published in 2009 by:
Nelson Thornes Ltd
Delta Place
27 Bath Road
CHELTENHAM
GL53 7TH
United Kingdom

10 11 12 13 / 10 9 8 7 6 5 4 3 2

A catalogue record for this book is available from the British Library

ISBN 978 0 7487 9870 4

Cover photograph: Alamy/Judith Collins

Page make-up by Thomson Digital Ltd

Printed in China by 1010 Printing International Ltd

Contents

Introduction

Nelson Thornes has worked in partnership with AQA to ensure this book and the accompanying online resources offer you the best support for your A Level course.

All resources have been approved by senior AQA examiners so you can feel assured that they closely match the specification for this subject and provide you with everything you need to prepare successfully for your exams.

These print and online resources together **unlock blended learning**; this means that the links between the activities in the book and the activities online blend together to maximise your understanding of a topic and help you achieve your potential.

These online resources are available on **kerboodle!** which can be accessed via the internet at **www.kerboodle.com/live**, anytime, anywhere. If your school or college subscribes to this service you will be provided with your own personal login details. Once logged in, access your course and locate the required activity.

For more information and help visit **www.kerboodle.com**

Icons in this book indicate where there is material online related to that topic. The following icons are used:

Learning activity

These resources include a variety of interactive and non-interactive activities to support your learning. These include online presentations of concepts from the student book, online case studies and interactive activities.

Progress tracking

These resources include a variety of tests that you can use to check your knowledge on particular topics (Test yourself) and a range of resources that enable you to analyse and understand examination questions (On your marks...).

Worked example

These resources provide step by step help on how to work through a particular accounting skill.

How to use this book

This book covers the specification for your course and is arranged in a sequence approved by AQA.

The book content is divided into chapters and topics that match the AQA Accounting specification for Units 3 and 4. Chapters 1–8 cover Unit 3 and chapters 9–16 cover Unit 4.

The features in this book include:

Learning objectives

At the beginning of each section you will find a list of learning objectives that contain targets linked to the requirements of the specification.

Key terms

Terms that you will need to be able to define and understand.

■ Illustration

A worked example that will show you how to go through a particular accounting skill.

■ Case Study

An overarching business scenario, to be used throughout a topic or a chapter.

■ Activity

Suggestions for practical investigations you can carry out, these will help you to test your knowledge and understanding.

■ Summary questions

Summary questions ...

■ Background Information

An extension to the main text that will provide you with added bits of useful knowledge.

■ Links

This highlights any areas where topics relate to another part of this book or the AS specification.

AQA Examiner's tip

Hints from AQA examiners to help you with your study and to prepare for your exam.

AQA Examination-style questions

Questions in the style that you can expect in your exam appear at the end of each topic and chapter.

Learning outcomes

Learning outcomes ...

■ International standards

The accounting specification for AQA now includes the international terminology as set by the International Accounting Standards. These terms have been incorporated into this textbook to enable you to become familiar with their use. Not only are the dual terms used within the chapter content but all of the past examination questions have been updated and rewritten using both the international term and the UK term, for example opening stock is now written as opening inventory (stock). Although both terms will be used within the examination questions it is expected that the UK term will be dropped in the future.

■ Synoptic content

Remember that the A2 examinations will include a question with content that is synoptic with the AS specification. This means that subject content from the AS will be assessed again within an A2 examination paper. The case study and chapter questions may therefore contain content from both the AS and A2 specification.

■ Web links in the book

As Nelson Thornes is not responsible for third party content online, there may be some changes to this material that are beyond our control. In order for us to ensure that the links referred to in the book are as up-to-date and stable as possible, the websites are usually homepages with supporting instructions on how to reach the relevant pages if necessary.

Please let us know at **kerboodle@nelsonthornes.com** if you find a link that doesn't work and we will do our best to redirect the link, or to find an alternative site.

UNIT 3

Further aspects of financial accounting

Introduction to Unit 3

Unit 3 is designed to develop your knowledge and understanding of financial accounting. You will find much of the work you undertook for the AS qualification will be of great value in this unit. For example, your understanding of accounting concepts and your ability to produce financial statements (final accounts) and balance sheets will prove invaluable as you develop skills in calculating the profit of businesses with limited accounting records, prepare accounting records for partnerships and study more advanced matters in relation to limited liability companies.

Chapter 1 – Sources of finance

You will look at some commonly used sources of finance for businesses, including bank loans and overdrafts, shares, debentures and internal finance. You will be expected to assess these types of finance, making appropriate recommendations as to which source to choose in particular circumstances.

Chapter 2 – Incomplete records

You will calculate the profits or losses of businesses which have not kept a full set of accounting records. You will learn a variety of techniques which are used to find the key information required to prepare financial statements under these circumstances. For example, you will learn how to calculate a business's credit sales when it has not maintained a sales day book or kept detailed records of trade receivables (debtors) in a sales ledger.

Chapter 3 – Partnerships accounts introduction

This chapter will introduce you to the accounting records of partnerships. You will learn how partners keep individual records of their investment in a business, and some of the techniques that can be used to share profits and losses between the partners. You will study certain aspects of the Partnership Act of 1890, and how this should be applied when partners have no agreement about how to share profits and losses.

Chapter 4 – Partnership and change in partners

You will develop your skills in preparing partnership accounts. You will learn how to record the retirement of a partner and the admission of a new partner. For the first time, you will develop an understanding of an intangible asset (goodwill) and learn how adjustments are made for this asset when there is a change in partners. You will study how to record the dissolution of a partnership (that is how to close down a partnership business) and work out how much should be paid to each partner after assets have been sold and liabilities discharged.

Chapter 5 – Published accounts of limited companies

You will develop your understanding of the accounts of limited liability companies by identifying the main elements of their published reports. You will see why companies are required to publish their accounts, the benefits to various users, but also gain an appreciation of the limitations of this process. You will also look at the duties of directors and contrast these with the duties of auditors.

Chapter 6 – Statements of cash flow

You will focus on a particular aspect of published accounts, i.e. statements of cash flow. You will develop skills in preparing these statements following the requirements of the relevant international accounting standard (IAS7). You will learn how to interpret statements of cash flow and how to assess the importance of these statements to others, particularly shareholders.

Chapter 7 – Accounting standards

You will learn about international accounting standards which are of great significance in ensuring that the financial statements prepared by companies are comparable, understandable and reliable. You will be looking at ten of these standards and the focus will be on gaining an insight into the purpose and importance of each standard. You will not be expected to have a detailed knowledge of each standard (except IAS 7 which concerns statements of cash flows).

Chapter 8 – Inventory (stock) valuation

You will focus your attention on inventory (stock). You will learn how to calculate inventory using two different methods, and you will also learn about the advantages and disadvantages of each of these methods. You will also learn to calculate a business's end of year inventory in situations where the valuation of the inventory has been delayed.

As you might expect, when you are assessed on this unit, you will be required to prepare financial statements, accounts, computations (i.e. annotated calculations). You will also, of course, be expected to write about accounting topics as well, providing explanations and reports in which you evaluate situations, giving advice and making recommendations. All the skills you developed preparing for the AS examination will now be very useful as you prepare for this module's assessment. For example, you will already know just how important it is to prepare accounting statements which are well presented and you will already have learned how to write effective explanations and reports. Do bear in mind, however, that many of the techniques you are mastering are more complex than those for the AS modules and that your prose answers will need to show a greater depth of understanding. Add to this the fact that, in general, higher standards are expected at A2 level.

1   Sources of finance

In this chapter you will learn how to:

- explain the advantages and disadvantages of a number of sources of finance (internal finance, shares, debentures, bank loans and overdrafts, and mortgages)

- apply understanding of types of finance to enable the most appropriate type of finance to be chosen in a particular situation

- evaluate different sources of finance and recommend the most appropriate choice to the owner(s) of a business.

Background information

Businesses require finance at all stages of their progress whatever their size and degree of success. As is often the case with individuals, the more successful a business, the easier it is to secure finance. Large, well-established businesses can borrow more and with better conditions attached, for example lower interest rates than would be available to a sole trader just starting out. Not all sources of finance are available to all types of businesses.

Key term

Internal finance: this is often the first source of finance for a business to consider and involves freeing up cash within the business.

The owners of businesses need to know the various sources of finance available in order to choose the one best suited to them and their situation. It is not necessarily the cheapest source of finance which is best. A business must consider the timescale involved and whether they are surrendering any control of the business in return for the finance. In order for you to be able to advise the owner(s) of the business about the different sources of finance and which is most appropriate, you need to understand what they are and the advantages and disadvantages of each source. Finance is needed for all sorts of reasons. At the start, finance will be needed to buy non-current (fixed) assets such as machinery, computers or delivery vehicles. There will also be marketing and, possibly, training to carry out and it is very unlikely a new business would instantly secure credit facilities with suppliers so they need to ensure they have enough finance to buy all the inventory (stock) they require. Once they are more established they may want to set up additional outlets or expand overseas. All of these decisions require finance.

What is internal finance?

Internal finance is when the owner of a business looks within the business for possible sources of finance.

Table 1 *Sources of internal finance*

Improving cash inflows	Reducing cash outflows
■ Tighter credit control; offer discounts for early payment and/or charge interest for late payment ■ Sell non-current (fixed) assets which are no longer required	■ Minimise wastage; how could this be done? ■ Tight inventory (stock) control, e.g. Just In Time (keeping stock to a minimum and only replacing inventory (stock) as it is sold) ■ Delay paying current liabilities (creditors) where possible

Retaining profit is an obvious means of finance for those businesses doing well. Profit is a measure of the performance of the business assessed at the end of the financial year, but that profit will have been generated by revenue (sales) transaction by transaction over the course of that year. The cash generated from these revenue (sales) transactions though will have flowed into and out of the company on a daily basis. Hence whilst the business may have made substantial profits it does not mean that there is physical cash in place that mirrors this profit as profit itself is not real, it is a measurement only. For example, a business can have made a large profit but have spent cash on purchasing new non-current (fixed) assets. The cost of the non-current (fixed) assets is spread over their useful life using depreciation. Any successful business would be wise to re-invest some profit made back into working capital and non-current (fixed) assets.

What are the advantages of internal finance?

No interest is paid and no loss of control outside of the business. For example a loan may be secured against a non-current (fixed) asset such as a vehicle which will be taken back by the company if the business cannot afford the repayments.

Any disadvantages?

■ There may be insufficient amounts for what you need to do.

■ May conflict with stakeholder wants. For example, shareholders want short-term profits for payment of dividends, managers want profit to be retained for investment and growth, employees may want profits to be used for pay rises or investment in training. Thus there are differing and diverse pressures for how any profits generated should be used.

■ **Case study**

Sources of finance for start-ups

Josie is a fitness fanatic and keen to set up her own gym just for women and strictly no mirrors. She has some savings and several friends and family who are supportive of her project. She is unsure where to get the finance required to buy the equipment she needs. She has found premises to rent but would want to buy her own site in the long term so that she has more control over how she uses the building. If successful she believes that she could turn her business into a national chain.

Ordinary shares

Only private limited companies (Ltd) and public limited companies (plc) can issue (sell) shares. Private limited companies sell their shares to friends, family and employees and as the word 'public' suggests for plcs these can be sold to anyone. Shares can provide large amounts of finance, a lump sum cash injection that never needs to be repaid and there is no need to pay **dividends**. However, you need to get your shareholders on your side if you decide not to pay dividends and explain why. Perhaps you need the finance to buy new premises which will result in higher profits in future years and subsequently larger dividends. If your shareholders are unconvinced by your reasoning then they may well sell their shares which could ultimately lead to a fall in share value if enough of them did this. The actual company has no direct influence over share value as this is led by supply and demand for the shares.

What are the advantages of ordinary shares?

If there is insufficient cash or profit or both then dividends do not have to be paid. Large amounts of money can be raised which does not have to be repaid.

What are the disadvantages of ordinary shares?

Loss of control: ordinary shareholders are the owners of the company. Some shareholders are not interested in the long-term future of the business and simply want to make a quick profit. This is why many

■ **Key term**

Dividends: this is the reward to the shareholders for investing. It is not guaranteed that dividends will be paid if there is insufficient cash or profit.

AQA Examiner's tip

If you need to decide on whether a business should pay out dividends it is essential to not only look at the profit but also the cash position. Just because a profit has been made it does not mean there will be cash as this could have already have been re-invested in non-current (fixed) assets.

businesses like their employees to own shares in the business because they will care about the future success. There is also the risk of takeover. This happens when a shareholder buys over 50% of the shares and so becomes the majority shareholder.

Preference shares

These shares have a preferential right to dividends over ordinary shareholders. This means that they will be paid their dividend first. They are considered to be lower risk for the investor because they are more likely to receive a dividend. However, their return is likely to be lower than that of an ordinary share. Holders of preference shares are not usually entitled to vote at the annual general meeting. **Preferences shares** can be cumulative or non-cumulative. If they are cumulative the dividend payout will build up even when there is no cash to pay out (this year it will be added to the following year). This means that if there is insufficient cash to pay out in one year in the second year the shareholder will receive the first year's dividends plus the current second year's dividends. This does not happen with non-cumulative.

Activity

 What are the advantages and disadvantages of preference shares for both the investor and the business?

Debentures

The most common error with **debentures** is that they are thought to be a type of share. They are actually a long-term loan and useful for financing projects that will take time to generate returns. The debenture holder lends the money for a fixed time period and a fixed amount of interest – for example, 7% debentures until 2025. This means that each year the debenture holder will receive 7% of the amount they have lent the company each year as interest and then in the year 2025 they will be repaid the original value in full. Debentures are useful when the business is certain they will then have the cash available in the necessary year to make the repayment as, unlike bank loans, only the interest is paid each year. Debenture interest is not optional and must be paid even when there is insufficient profit and/or cash. Debenture holders may be concerned about the risk they are taking in lending the money to the business in which case the debentures are secured against the assets and the term 'mortgage' debenture is used. If the debentures are not secured they are simple or naked debentures.

Bank loans

Bank loans could be arranged for a medium term, up to ten years or a long term over ten years. This source of finance is often used to purchase non-current (fixed) assets or for a specific project. The **loan** may be secured on the asset which has been bought with the funds raised by the loan and then if the business is unable to repay the loan this asset will be seized and used to pay the outstanding amount. Each month or year interest and part of the loan will be repaid. This can simplify budgeting as you know exactly how much you will be paying if the interest is fixed. Loans are not as flexible as overdrafts as you may not be able to make overpayments during times when you have surplus cash and if you can then there may be a penalty charge involved.

AQA Examiner's tip

You need to make sure you are examining the source of finance from the correct viewpoint. This is particularly important when considering **risk**. From a business point of view ordinary shares may be low risk as they do not have to pay dividends whereas for the ordinary shareholder you may consider them fairly high risk as you may not get a return on your investment. A common error is for candidates to answer questions from, for example, the shareholders' perspective when the question was looking at finance from the business's viewpoint. Take time to read the question carefully to avoid this.

Key terms

Preference shares: for shareholders these are a lower risk option to ordinary shares but as a consequence offer a lower return.

Debentures: these are loans by debenture holders who receive interest for the term of the debenture. They must not be confused with shares.

Bank loans: borrowing a fixed sum over a fixed term which can be secured on assets in the business or unsecured. Interest must be paid in addition to the amount borrowed.

AQA Examiner's tip

If you are asked to assess the suitable sources of finance for a business it is essential that, after having weighed up the pros and cons of the potential sources, you then reach a final decision and justify that. You may well decide that a combination of sources is best. If so, explain why.

Link

Types of business organisation is studied in AS Accounting (Unit 2).

Key terms

Bank overdrafts: represent a flexible source of finance and mean a business can spend more than they have in their bank account within a set limit.

Mortgages: these are long-term loans specifically for purchasing property.

Risk: all lenders have to decide on the level of risk a business presents. This is based on past experience, future predictions and on the current state of the business. The lender must decide how likely they are to be repaid and whether the likely return is worth the potential risk. In the role of the borrower, the business also has to weigh up the risks of any source of finance. The business must consider its financial needs, as well as the implications associated with each source.

Ordinary shares: these are the most common type of share issued. An ordinary shareholder receives a variable dividend based on profit in return for their investment.

AQA **Examiner's tip**

It is easier for both you and the examiner if you consider one source of finance at a time rather than completing advantages of them all and then revisiting them for the disadvantages.

AQA **Examiner's tip**

Remember, some sources of finance will clearly be inappropriate for a business, such as a sole trader issuing shares, but in other circumstances there may be several possible sources which could be of use. You must match the source to its use.

Bank overdrafts

A **bank overdraft** is the most common type of short-term finance. It provides useful cash and is often the cheapest form of borrowing as, although the interest rate is usually higher than a bank loan, you are only charged interest when actually overdrawn. It is essential that a close eye is kept on the limit set as banks will charge higher interest and fees for exceeding it. Although we consider overdrafts as short term many businesses are frequently overdrawn each month if their cash flow is not always consistent. Overdrafts are often used for day-to-day expenses rather than large capital expenditure and are seen by many businesses as a safety net. They are flexible as they can be repaid when the business wants to.

Mortgages

Mortgages are obtained for purchasing premises. The amount lent and the interest rate will vary according to the premises involved and the financial record of the business. They are a long-term liability and usually a relatively cheap source of finance. They are particularly useful for smaller businesses who may struggle to borrow elsewhere as a mortgage is secured against their premises making it a lower risk for the lender, who can repossess (take back the property by force using a court order) if the borrower defaults.

Activities

2 In groups you need to split the sources of finance between you and research what they are and the advantages and disadvantages of each. You can then compile a group handout of your findings. Evaluate which would be the best sources for Josie starting her gym. She intends to start as a sole trader.

3 Imran, an old friend from college, has approached Josie as he thinks she has found a new and expanding market and wants to join her. What sources of finance could now be available?

Risks in being a lender or borrower

Risk is important to both the lender and borrower. The lender or investor wants to ensure they receive a return on their funds and ultimately repayment. The business, in the role of borrower, wants an affordable option but also the source of finance to be in a form and length of time appropriate for their needs. The business also needs to weigh up factors like losing control, for example, by issuing **ordinary shares**. Shareholders usually want to see a good return on their investment whilst the original owners may wish to use retained profit to expand the business further, for example, by buying additional non-current (fixed) assets. Most businesses will require sources of finance at some stage of their existence. What you need to examine is the type of business, what the finance is being used for and the financial situation the business finds itself in.

In this chapter you will have learnt:

- the advantages and disadvantages which arise from each of the sources of finance
- to apply understanding of each source so as to be able to choose the most appropriate source of finance for a particular situation.

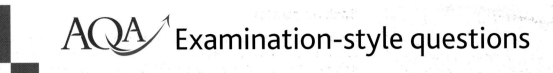

AQA Examination-style questions

1   Distinguish between debentures and ordinary shares.

2   Harvey and Bailey are in partnership. Explain the additional sources of finance they could benefit from by becoming a limited company.

3   Creamy Smoothies Ltd wants to expand into the European market. They have two factories, a healthy profit from the past year and approximately £5,000 cash at bank. They estimate they require £125,000 for their plans. Discuss how best they should raise the finance.

4   Discuss the possible conflict which may exist between the managers and shareholders of a company when raising finance.

2 Incomplete records

This chapter prepares you to answer incomplete records questions which often appear daunting as it can be difficult to assess what information is of use to you and where it should be placed. In the first topic we will start by looking at why incomplete records occur and how a statement of affairs can be produced to help calculate profit or loss without the need to complete an income statement (profit and loss account). Incomplete records are more common in businesses owned by sole traders but they also could occur in partnerships. The second topic, preparing financial statements (final accounts) and balance sheets for businesses with incomplete records, brings together previous techniques you have completed at AS level. It is possible to produce a set of final accounts without a complete trial balance and you will learn how to do this by the end of this chapter.

Topic 1 Calculating profits and losses from changes in capital

In this topic you will learn how to:

- assess the profit or loss made by a business which has minimal accounting records based on a comparison of the value of capital at two different dates

- evaluate a system of incomplete records based on comparing capitals comparing this with full accounting systems.

The reasons for incomplete records

Incomplete records range from partially completed accounts to a list of assets and a pile of bank statements. A sole trader or partnership often has neither the time nor expertise to keep a double entry bookkeeping system. Preparing accounting statements is essential for tax purposes and for making effective management decisions. With the price of computers and software packages specifically for accounts becoming more cost effective, it is increasingly easier for a non-accountant to keep basic records. This will then keep accountancy fees lower when the end of year accounts need to be prepared.

Limited companies would usually employ a bookkeeper and larger companies have whole departments with a range of accounting staff but – although keeping financial records – these employees may not have the qualifications to produce a full set of final accounts. Many accounting software packages are generic, so unless the business pays for a tailor-made package the system may only complete some of the required record keeping. Some sole traders might use a single entry system. This involves recording all payments, receipts and other transactions in one cash book. This is helpful but we still need to draw out items such as drawings and capital expenditure. Capital expenditure, spending or improving on non-current (fixed) assets means that we need to calculate depreciation. Adjustments for other trade payables (trade creditors) and other trade receivables (prepayments) will also need to be made.

Advantages of maintaining limited accounting records

- Simple and easy to do, particularly for small businesses that may not have financial expertise.

- Do not need to hire a permanent fully qualified accountant.
- Do not need expensive tailor-made accounting software.

Statement of affairs

In order to calculate the capital at the beginning of the financial year, we use the accounting equation:

$$\text{assets} - \text{liabilities} = \text{capital}$$

Statement of Affairs for J. Wimpenny at 1 January 2008

	£	£
Assets		
Machinery		10,000
Inventory (stock)		2,000
Trade receivables (trade debtors)		1,000
Bank		5,500
		18,500
Liabilities		
Trade payables (trade creditors)	3,500	
Other payables (accruals)	500	4,000
Capital		14,500

Fig. 2.1 *An example of a statement of affairs*

Total assets – total liabilities = capital

$18,500 - 4,000 = £14,500$

So, we can calculate that at 1 January 2008, J. Wimpenny had £14,500 invested in his business.

It is a useful to complete a **statement of affairs** if we do not have a balance sheet for the previous year.

Case study

Sundip Patel

Sundip Patel is a games software designer who is involved in generating the backgrounds on virtual online games. He enjoys his work and although he is more than capable of maintaining accounting records he considers it to be a waste of his time. Sundip is starting to have to turn away projects because he is unable to keep up with the demand for his service.

Using a statement of affairs to calculate profit or loss

It is possible to calculate profit without a trading income statement (profit and loss account). Unless capital has been introduced, the only

Activity

1 In pairs, discuss which accounting concepts need to be considered when an incomplete set of accounting records have been maintained.

Key term

Statement of affairs: this is a basic balance sheet which can be used to calculate missing figures such as profit, loss, opening or closing capital.

Activities

2 Outline the reasons why Sundip does not currently maintain full accounting records.

3 Explain two benefits Sundip could gain from keeping accounting records.

way capital can increase over the year is by profit being earned. You need to first calculate the opening and closing capital balances using two statements of affairs, for the start and the end of the year and then you are able to compare them to find any increase or decrease in capital which would represent profit or loss made over the period.

Illustration

Calculating profit or loss using opening and closing capital

Assets or liabilities	At 30 March 2008	At 30 March 2009
Premises	100,000	120,000
Vehicles	30,000	25,000
Inventory (stock)	2,000	2,500
Trade receivables (trade debtors)	1,800	1,950
Trade payables (trade creditors)	880	1,020
Long-term bank loan	20,000	18,000

Fig. 2.2 *Assets and liabilities*

Sundip Patel presented us with the above information. The opening capital as at 30 March 2008 is £112,920. We find this by totalling the assets (100,000 + 30,000 + 2,000 + 1,800) and then subtracting the liabilities (880 + 20,000). If we do the same for 2009 we find the closing capital to be £130,430: assets (120,000 + 25,000 + 2,500 + 1,950) £149,450 less liabilities (1,020 + 18,000) £19,020.

Closing capital − opening capital = profit or loss

£130,430 − £112,920 = £17,510 profit

However, it is likely that the owner will have had drawings of either inventory (stock) or cash during the year and possibly have introduced additional capital. In this case we need to adjust capital using a layout such as the following one:

	£
Closing capital	
Less opening capital	
Add drawings	
Less capital introduced	
Profit for the year	

Fig. 2.3 *Adjusting capital*

Activity

4 Complete the above table using Sundip's previous information. He has also introduced £5,000 which was an inheritance and has drawings of £10,000.

Assessment: using a statement of affairs to calculate profit or loss

This is a quick method to discover profit or loss without completing a income statement (full trading, profit and loss account). It is accurate as long as the figures provided are accurate, such as the trade receivables (trade debtors), trade payables (trade creditors), inventory (stock), etc.

Drawbacks

1 The method is not detailed enough for management purposes.
2 It would not be sufficient for income tax and VAT purposes.

Activity

5 Sundip's friend is a trainee accountant and considers that Sundip should complete a full set of accounting records in order to calculate profit or loss rather than comparing capitals. Advise Sundip as to whether his friend is correct.

In this topic you will have learnt:

- how to prepare a statement of affairs and calculate profit or loss from changes in capital over time
- how to assess the drawbacks of maintaining limited accounting records.

 **Examiner's tip**

If you are just told to calculate the profit then this should be possible using the method described in this chapter rather than preparing a full profit and loss account. Read the wording carefully so that you are aware of the requirements and do not waste time preparing unnecessary answers.

AQA Examiner's tip

A common problem with incomplete records is a failure to give detailed workings which show how missing figures were obtained. A significant number of marks will be available for workings so you must take the time to show clear workings.

 # AQA Examination-style questions

1 Examine the purpose of a statement of affairs.

2 Dermot Reegan is a car mechanic and supplies you with the following information:

	1 January 2008 £	31 December 2008 £
Premises	120,000	120,000
Vehicles	50,000	60,000
Machinery	12,000	30,000
Bank	1,300	1,800
Cash	500	650
Trade payables (trade creditors)	2,000	1,800
Trade receivables (trade debtors)	3,300	3,750
Inventory (stock)	1,200	1,500

Required

Calculate the profit or loss for the year taking into account Dermot's drawings of £10,000.

3   AQA January 2003 past exam question

Sharon Segg started a woodworking business on 1 December 2001 with net assets valued at £87,000.

She has been so busy she did not keep any financial records during the year. However, Sharon is able to give you the following information as at 30 November 2002.

	£
Premises at valuation	47,000
Machinery at net book value	21,600
Van at net book value	12,000
Money owed by customers	1,090
Money owed to suppliers	7,450
Inventory (stock) of timber, etc.	5,700
Bank overdraft	640

During the year Sharon withdrew £9,450 in cash from the business for her private use. She also used timber valued at £2,100 to make improvements to her home.

Required

(a)   Calculate her profit for the year ended 30 November 2002.

(b)   Evaluate the advantages and disadvantages of the method that you used to determine net profit.

4   AQA Summer 2005

Tom's opening capital on 1 March 2003 was £32,000.

His assets and liabilities at 29 February 2004 were:

	£
Machinery at valuation	46,000
Two vehicles at valuation	34,000
Loan from Eliza, a friend	20,000
Inventory (stock) of cleaning materials	380
Amounts outstanding for the purchase of cleaning materials	180
Amounts owed by customers	1,870
Bank balance	640

During the year, Tom:

took £14,184 cash from the business for his private use; took cleaning materials to the value of £96 for use in his home; received a gift of £15,000 from his mother, which he paid into his business bank account.

Calculate Tom's profit for the year ended 29 February 2004.

5   Rebecca Chappell owns a children's nursery and supplies the following information:

	31 December 2008	31 December 2009
Premises	120,000	130,000
Equipment	10,000	15,000
Cash	1,000	1,500
Bank	2,225	3,800
Inventory (stock)	275	122
Trade receivables (trade debtors)	987	1,030
Other receivables (prepayments)	250	300
Trade payables (trade creditors)	760	550

During the year ended 31 December 2009 Rebecca introduced her bingo winnings of £2,500 and took £80 worth of stock home for her own children's use.

Calculate Rebecca's profit for the year.

Topic 2   Preparing financial statements (final accounts) and balance sheets for businesses with incomplete records

In this topic you will learn how to:

- prepare the financial accounts (final accounts) and balance sheet of a business which has incomplete accounting records

- use a variety of techniques to calculate key figures for inclusion in the final accounts and balance sheet of a business which has incomplete accounting records

- use more advanced techniques to calculate missing cash or inventory (stock)

- evaluate this system of incomplete records comparing it with full accounting systems.

Credit revenue (sales) and credit purchases

Cash revenue (sales) and purchases can usually be calculated by looking at the cash book, till rolls and receipts. However, when calculating credit revenue (sales) and purchases debtor balances and creditor balances must be taken account of at both the beginning and end of the year.

Essential information to calculate credit revenue (sales) and credit purchases:

Table 1 *Information required*

Credit revenue (sales)	Credit purchases
Opening balance of trade receivables (trade debtors)	Opening balance of trade payables (trade creditors)
Closing balance of trade receivables (trade debtors)	Closing balance of trade payables (trade creditors)
Receipts from trade receivables (trade debtors)	Payments to trade payables (trade creditors)

We can calculate credit revenue (sales) and credit purchases by completing a revenue (sales) ledger or purchase ledger control account with the known information and then calculating the missing figures. It might also be necessary to consider: discounts received, discounts allowed, bad debts, returns inwards, returns outwards, interest charged to debtors or finance costs (interest) charged by trade payables (creditors).

■ Illustration

How to set out a revenue (sales) ledger control account or revenue (sales) totals account

Dr			Revenue (sales) ledger control account					Cr
			£					£
Dec	1	Bal b/d	20,000	Dec	31	Receipts from debtors		62,000
	31	**Revenue (sales)**	**86,050**		31	Revenue (sales) returns		2,000
	31	Interest charged	1,000		31	Discounts allowed		3,250
					31	Bad debts		500
					31	Bal c/d		39,300
			107,050					107,050
Jan	1	Bal b/d	39,300					

Fig. 2.4 *Revenue (sales) ledger control account*

Remember that the opening debtors balance is a DEBIT, DD (debit debtors) may help you to remember which side to start on. Entries on the debit side increase the amount the debtors owe you. The control account is then completed and the total of credit revenue (sales) from the revenue (sales) day book can be calculated by filling in the missing figure. In this case the missing revenue (sales) figure is £86,050.

For a purchase ledger control account, purchase totals account is used to find credit purchases, see below:

Dr			Purchase ledger control account					Cr
			£					£
Dec	31	Payments to trade payables (trade creditors)	93,500	Dec	1	Bal b/d		62,000
	31	Purchase returns	3,000		31	**Purchases**		**112,500**
	31	Discounts received	4,200		31	Interest paid		990
	31	Bal c/d	74,790		31			
			175,490					175,490
				Jan	1	Bal b/d		74,790

Fig. 2.5 *Purchase ledger control account*

This time the balance brought down is CREDIT, CC (credit creditors) for trade payables (trade creditors). Again, total credit purchases from the purchases day book can be calculated. In this case the missing figure is £112,500.

Calculating missing figures using mark up or margin

Many businesses, especially sole traders, use a simple system of adding a set percentage mark up to their goods or services so they know that they are making a profit margin on everything they sell. We can use this information to calculate revenue (sales) or the cost of revenue (sales) if these figures are not supplied. The important distinction to make here is that margin is a percentage profit based on the selling price and mark up is based on the cost of revenue (sales).

Mark up

This is when a set percentage is added to the cost to generate the revenue (sales) value.

▇ Illustration

If you know the cost of revenue (sales) and the mark up is 10%:

£60,000 + 10% of cost of revenue (sales) = £66,000 revenue (sales)

If you know the revenue (sales) and want to find the cost of revenue (sales), then $\dfrac{66,000}{1.1}$ = £60,000 cost of revenue (sales)

If the percentage was 20% then you would divide by 1.2 and so on.

▇ Illustration

How to prepare a trading account

Dawid Jurkiewicz runs a joke shop selling a range of items. The following information is given on 30 November 2008.

Opening inventory (stock) at cost	£50,000
Mark up on cost	20%
Rate of inventory (stock) turnover	8 times
Closing inventory (stock)	£55,000

Fig. 2.6 *Information supplied*

You are required to prepare the trading account for the year ended 30 November 2008.

Trading account for Dawid Jurkiewicz for the year ended 30 November 2008

		£	£
Revenue (sales)			504,000
Less	**Cost of revenue (sales)**		
	Opening inventory (stock)	50,000	
	Purchases	425,000	
	Closing inventory (stock)	55,000	
			420,000
	Gross profit		84,000

Fig. 2.7 *Trading account to show mark-up method*

Start by entering the information which you are sure about which is the opening and closing stock. We can then use the rate of inventory (stock) turnover to calculate the cost of revenue (sales).

$$\text{Cost of revenue (sales)} = \frac{\text{opening inventory (stock)} + \text{closing inventory (stock)} \times \text{inventory (stock) turnover}}{2}$$

So, $420,000 = \dfrac{50,000 + 55,000 \times 8}{2}$

Then add the closing inventory (stock) of £55,000 to the cost of revenue (sales) of £420,000 and subtract the opening stock of £50,000 to find the purchases of £425,000. To find the gross profit calculate 20% of the cost of revenue (sales) £420,000 which is £84,000 and add the two amounts together to find the revenue (sales) of £504,000.

Margin

This is when a fixed percentage profit margin is made on every sale, i.e. 10% is profit and 90% of the sales revenue made is cost of revenue (sales), so revenue (sales) × 0.9 = cost of revenue (sales).

■ **Illustration**

If you know the revenue (sales) are £90,000 and the margin is 10% then:

90,000 × 10% = £9,000 profit

Cost of revenue (sales) is the revenue (sales) – profit = £90,000 = £81,000

Alternatively, £90,000 – 10% = £81,000; this is the same as £90,000 × 0.9 = £81,000

So, if you know the cost of revenue (sales) and the fixed percentage profit margin, you can work out the revenue (sales):

$\dfrac{81,000}{0.9}$ = £90,000 revenue (sales)

To obtain the 0.9 think about 10% subtracted from 100% and put a decimal point in, so, 20% converts to 0.8.

■ **Illustration**

Michelle Roberts owns a pie shop specialising in unusual meat. The following information is given on 31 July 2008.

Revenue (sales)	£100,000
Gross profit margin	40%
Rate of inventory (stock) turnover	20 times
Opening inventory (stock)	£5,000

Fig. 2.8 *Information supplied*

You are required to prepare the trading account for the year ended 31 July 2008.

Trading account for Michelle Roberts for the year ended 31 July 2008

		£	£
Revenue (sales)			100,000
Less	Cost of revenue (sales)		
	Opening inventory (stock)	5,000	
	Purchases	56,000	
	Closing inventory (stock)	1,000	
			60,000
	Gross profit		40,000

Fig. 2.9 *Trading account to show margin method*

Again, start by entering the information which you are sure about which is the opening inventory (stock) and revenue (sales). This time use the revenue (sales) figure to calculate gross profit by finding 40% of revenue (sales) which is £40,000. Subtract the gross profit from the revenue (sales) to find cost of revenue (sales) of £60,000.

$$\text{Cost of revenue (sales)} = \frac{\text{opening inventory (stock)} + \text{closing inventory (stock)} \times \text{inventory (stock) turnover}}{2}$$

$$\text{So } 60,000 = \frac{5,000 + \text{closing inventory (stock)} \times 20}{2}$$

Divide £60,000 by 20 to find £3,000 which represents the average stock so closing inventory (stock) must be £1,000 so that 5,000 + 1,000 divided by 2 is £3,000. To find purchases start with the cost of revenue (sales) of £60,000 add the closing inventory (stock) of £1,000 and subtract the opening inventory (stock) of £5,000.

Inventory (stock) losses

If inventory (stock) is lost because of fire or theft then it must be valued in order to make an insurance claim or account for the loss on the final accounts. Even if inadequate inventory (stock) records were kept we can still value the stock loss by constructing a trading account and using the mark up or margin technique.

Illustration

Kay owns a balloon shop in the local high street and on 21 May there was a fire which destroyed most of her inventory (stock). She could salvage £500 worth and the insurance assessor requires an accurate assessment of inventory (stock) loss on the claim form.

At the start of the financial year Kay had an opening inventory (stock) value of £6,000. Her purchases to 21 May had been £28,000. Her revenue (sales) to this date were £40,000, Kay has a margin of 25% on revenue (sales).

AQA Examiner's tip

Extract the figures you definitely know when completing an incomplete records question and then look for the gaps you need to complete.

Activities

6 Calculate the revenue (sales) and gross profit if the cost of revenue (sales) is £360,000 with a 20% mark up.

7 Calculate the cost of revenue (sales) and gross profit if the revenue (sales) are £20,000 with a 25% mark up.

8 Calculate the cost of revenue (sales) and gross profit if the revenue (sales) are £400,000 with a gross profit margin of 25%.

9 Calculate the revenue (sales) and gross profit if the cost of revenue (sales) is £260,000 with a 35% gross profit margin.

Trading account for Kay for the period ended 21 May 2008

		£	£
Revenue (sales)			40,000
Less	**Cost of revenue (sales)**		
	Opening inventory (stock)	6,000	
	Purchases	28,000	
	Closing inventory (stock)	**4,000**	30,000
	Gross profit		10,000

Fig. 2.10 *Trading account to show loss of inventory (stock)*

So, if revenue (sales) = £40,000 and revenue (sales) margin = 25% then gross profit = £10,000. If revenue (sales) = £40,000 and profit was £10,000 then the cost of revenue (sales) = £30,000. From this we can now find the missing figure representing the inventory (stock) Kay should have had. This is done by calculating what closing inventory (stock) should have been by laying our information out in a trading account. We can see that the closing inventory (stock) should have been £4,000 and if Kay now has only £500 worth of inventory (stock) left then £3,500 was lost in the fire.

In the trading account, when calculating the cost of revenue (sales), the closing inventory (stock) must include any missing inventory (stock) so that gross profit can be calculated. The missing inventory (stock) should not be included on the balance sheet as we do not have it so it cannot be an asset. If Kay is not insured then missing inventory (stock) is written off as an expense on the profit and loss account. If she does have adequate insurance then it will appear as a current asset on the balance sheet until the insurance company pays her.

Calculation of missing cash

Exam questions sometimes require you to calculate a cash figure due to a theft. The key here is to prepare a cash account based on what should have happened and then compare it with the actual position.

■ Illustration

Sundip Patel does not keep a full set of accounting records. Whilst in a café-bar after visiting several clients Sundip had his briefcase stolen containing cash which he was on his way to deposit at the bank, but he was unsure of how much. He can provide the following information:

	£
Cash balance at 1 July 2008	278
Cash balance at 30 June 2009	145
Cash revenue (sales) for the year	34,525
Cash paid into the bank during the year	30,250
Expenses paid by cash	2,870

Fig. 2.11 *Information supplied*

Dr			Cash				Cr	
			£				£	
June	30	Bal b/d	278	June	30	Bank	30,250	
	30	Revenue (sales)	34,525		30	Expenses	2,870	
					30	**Stolen**	**1,538**	
					30	Bal c/d	145	
			34,803				34,803	
July	1	Bal b/d	145					

Fig. 2.12 *Cash account*

By completing all the known figures first, we can then work out how much has been stolen from Sundip. In this case the figure is £1,538.

Stages in completing final accounts from incomplete records

The approach will vary according to the information given:

1 If you do know the assets and liabilities at the start or end of the year then you can complete a statement of affairs in order to calculate the opening and/or closing capital.

2 When completing control (totals) accounts, be careful – payments to trade payables (trade creditors) and receipts from trade receivables (trade debtors) do not represent sales and purchases. You must take into account opening and closing trade receivables (trade debtors) and trade payables (trade creditors).

3 Use mark up or margin as appropriate, mark up is based on cost of sales and margin is based on sales.

4 If you are told inventory (stock) turnover then you can use this to calculate the cost of sales:

$$\text{Cost of revenue (sales)} = \frac{(\text{opening inventory (stock)} + \text{closing inventory (stock)}) \times \text{inventory (stock) turnover}}{2}$$

Revenue (sales) can also be found by applying any mark up or margin information to the cost of revenue (sales) figure.

5 Draw up the outline of the final accounts and include as much information as you can find remembering to take account of other payables (accruals) and other receivables (prepayments), adjustments to drawings etc. For example, last year's other payables (accruals) should have been paid last year and so need subtracting and this year's other payables (accruals) need adding. Ask yourself what costs and revenues actually happened in this accounting period rather than when were they paid. Remember profit is calculated using the other payables (accruals) concept. Include both cash revenue (sales) and credit revenue (sales) in the revenue (sales) figure and the same for purchases.

In this topic you will have learnt:

■ how to calculate credit revenue (sales) and purchases figures using total accounts

■ how to calculate missing figures using mark up or margin

■ how to prepare and comment on financial statements (final accounts) based on incomplete records.

AQA Examiner's tip

Don't forget to include the cash and/or bank account when calculating opening or closing capital amounts as these are sometimes shown separately to the other information.

Link

In AS Unit 1 you will have learnt how to perform a bank reconciliation, this could be useful for an incomplete records question where perhaps the bank balance is unknown due to a lack of cash book and should be revised.

Link

Gross profit margin, mark up and rate of stock turnover were all studied as part of AS Unit 2.

AQA Examiner's tip

You must show detailed workings on your answer paper and not on the exam paper. There are marks available which you should maximise.

 Examination-style questions

1 Max Turner is a sole trader and operates as an antiques dealer. The following details relate to his business for the year ended 31 March 2009.

Revenue (sales)	£900,000
Gross profit margin	25%
Rate of inventory (stock) turnover	10 times
Opening inventory (stock)	£40,000

Required

Prepare the trading account for the year ended 31 March 2009.

2 AQA January 2005

Pat Parker is a butcher. She marks up all goods sold in her shop by 100%. All takings are banked each evening after the shop is closed. During the year ended 31 December 2004, £93,322 was banked. Pat believes that some cash is missing from the till on 31 December 2004. She is unable to determine the exact amount but provides the following information.

	£
Inventory (stock) at 1 January 2004	890
Inventory (stock) at 31 December 2004	950
Purchases	46,753
Trade receivables (trade debtors) at 1 January 2004	2,786
Trade receivables (trade debtors) at 31 December 2004	2,640

Calculate the amount of cash missing from the till on 31 December 2004.

3 Kia Ng has not kept adequate records for his business for the year ended 30 June 2009. He has supplied the following information.

Mark up on cost	25%
Amount paid to trade payables (trade creditors)	£363,000
Business expenses (excluding depreciation)	£52,100
Drawings	£20,500

	30 June 2008	30 June 2009
Vehicle	12,000	10,000
Cash at bank	3,300	4,200
Trade payables (creditors)	8,000	6,500
Inventory (stock)	6,000	12,000
Prepaid business expenses	220	450

Required

(a) Prepare the trading, profit and loss account for the year ended 30 June 2009.

(b) Prepare a balance sheet as at 30 June 2009.

(c) Evaluate the problems of Kia not keeping adequate accounting records.

4 AQA Summer 2006

Michael Wong is the proprietor of a retail gift shop. He has one outlet and a small warehouse where he keeps his stock. Michael does not keep full accounting records, but he is able to provide the following information for the year ended 31 March 2006.

	£	Cash account	£
1 April 2005 bal b/fwd	784	Payments to current liabilities (creditors)	178,943
Cash banked	253,641	Warehouse rent	7,800
Received from debtors	2,356	Advertising and wrapping materials	12,340
		Rates and insurances	11,870
		Purchase of vehicle	30,000
		Motor expenses	12,659
31 March 2006 bal c/fwd	4,393	General expenses	7,562
	261,174		261,174
		1 April 2006 bal b/fwd	4,393

Assets and liabilities	at 1 April 2005	at 31 March 2006
Premises	103,600	100,800
Fixtures and fittings	12,000	10,000
Vehicles	20,000	28,500
Inventory (stock)	4,562	4,328
Trade payables (trade creditors)	12,403	11,987
Trade receivables (trade debtors)	458	476
Warehouse rent unpaid	700	-
Insurances paid in advance	760	840
Cash at bank	784	-
Bank overdraft	-	4,393
Cash in hand	260	320

During March 2006 one of the vehicles, with a value of £12,000, was involved in an accident. The vehicle and all of the goods being carried in the vehicle had to be written off. The goods had cost £1,560. The insurance company agreed to pay £7,200 for the loss of the vehicle; the payment was made at the end of April 2006.

Unfortunately, Michael was not insured for the loss of the goods.

On 1 September 2005, a new vehicle was purchased for £30,000.

Before paying the shop takings into the bank account, Michael used some of the cash received to pay the following: cash for personal use £1,500 per calendar month, staff wages £2,650 per calendar month.

During December 2005, Michael took goods costing £368 from inventory (stock) to give as Christmas presents to his friends and relatives.

Required

(a)   Prepare the following accounts for the year ended 31 March 2006:

     i   a cash account

     ii a total trade receivables (debtors) account (control account)

     iii a total trade payables (creditors) account (control account)

     iv a vehicles account.

(b)   Prepare an income statement (trading and profit and loss account) for the year ended 31 March 2006.

3 Partnership accounts introduction

The next two chapters are concerned with partnerships. This topic forms a significant part of the specification. There are several areas you could be asked about so it is important you are confident with all of the techniques required as you could be asked about any area. The Partnership Act of 1890 defines partnership as 'the relationship which subsists between persons carrying on business with a view to a profit'. Partnerships still have unlimited liability so you have to trust your partners or you could be faced with losing your personal assets if the partnership fails, that is the decisions made by one partner are legally binding on the others even if these decisions are poorly made and lead the partnership into potential debt. This is known as joint and several liability. A partnership may be formed because there is too much work for a sole trader or because they want to be able to expand and need finance and expertise from elsewhere.

Topic 1   Sharing profits and losses

In this topic you will learn how to:

- explain the likely nature of agreements between partners in regard to sharing profits and losses
- apply the terms of the Partnership Act 1890 in regard to profit sharing
- prepare income statement (profit and loss appropriation accounts) for partnerships based on profit sharing agreements or on the terms of the Partnership Act 1890
- describe the purpose of fixed capital and current accounts
- prepare fixed capital and current accounts.

Partnerships are similar to sole traders in that the partners have unlimited liability so could potentially lose their personal assets if the partnership were to end with debts. Many of the disadvantages of being a sole trader are solved by forming a partnership such as greater capital introduced, more ideas and cover during holidays and sickness. Twenty was the maximum number of partners permitted by the law but that restriction has been removed and now partnerships vary in size from two to many hundreds. Accountants and solicitors have always been able to have in excess of twenty partners since due to their profession they are unable to have the security of limited liability, where the actual individuals do not lose personal assets. Limited liability partnerships do exist but our concern is with partnerships with unlimited liability.

Table 1 *Advantages and disadvantages of partnerships*

Advantages of being a partnership	Disadvantages of being a partnership
Additional capital introduced	Unlimited liability
Can share the workload and specialise	Potential disagreements
Variety of ideas and solutions to problems	Share profits
Cover for holidays or sick leave	

Link

You will have previously studied partnerships as part of AS Unit 2. This is useful background information for this topic.

Key terms

Deed of partnership: is a legal document, ideally all partnerships should have one of these so they know exactly how profits will be shared etc.

Interest on capital: is an appropriation of the profits of the partnership and rewards those partners who have invested most.

Partnership salary: this is a payment to a partner and appears in the appropriation section, not with expenses. It also is entered in the partner's current account. It may reflect that some partners may contribute more working hours than others.

Interest on drawings: in order to deter partners from taking excessive drawings there may be interest charged which is then debited to the partners' accounts.

Partnership Act 1890: this states, for example, how to share profits or losses if no agreement is in place.

Partnership agreements

It is usual for a partnership to draw up a written agreement such as a **deed of partnership** which sets out the terms and financial arrangements. This avoids disagreements at a later stage. This is a legally binding document.

Possible contents of a partnership agreement

In addition to the obvious information such as personal details of the partners, the decision-making process, working hours, etc., the following should be considered when drawing up a partnership agreement:

1 Capital introduced – how much each partner is required to contribute to the business.
2 Profit/loss sharing ratio – this is how the partners share the profits or losses and can be done according to who works the most hours, who is the most skilled, who contributed most capital etc.
3 **Interest on capital** – this is interest paid to the partners according to how much capital they have invested. The more they have invested, the more interest they receive. This reduces the amount of profit in the partnership but improves the individual partner's current account.
4 **Partnership salaries** – it may be agreed that some partners receive a salary in addition to their share of the profit or loss. This could be to ensure a partner receives a minimum income, perhaps because they left a lucrative salary with a company to join the partnership.
5 Drawings and **interest on drawings** – drawings is the amount which the partners withdraw from the partnership. Interest may be charged in order to minimise the amount removed. A serious cash shortage could be caused if one or more partners draws out a significant amount of cash.
6 Guarantees – if one partner guarantees that another will earn a minimum income in the business, such a guarantee should be written into the agreement.
7 Interest on loans – a partner may wish to lend the partnership finance as this could be a cheaper interest rate rather than using a financial institution.

If no partnership agreement exists then the **Partnership Act 1890** comes into effect which states that:

- profits and losses are shared equally
- there are no partners' salaries
- partners are entitled to 5% interest on any loans advanced to the business
- partners should not receive any interest on capital
- no interest on drawings.

Case study

Wenches with wrenches

Bonnie is a plumber operating as a sole trader who has captured a niche market in Guildford by completing jobs for women who would rather have another woman in their house to complete work needed. She has become very successful by completing jobs in the designated time frame and has a good reputation for tidying up after herself. She is having to turn jobs away and has been approached by Lucinda, a young woman who has just completed her plumbing qualifications, with the offer of a partnership.

Activities

1 Discuss whether Bonnie should enter into partnership with Lucinda.

2 Outline what details they should have in their partnership agreement.

Fixed capital accounts

Some partnerships may have fluctuating capital accounts where all entries associated with the actual partners are recorded. This does not reveal if one partner is drawing out considerably more than the others. This can be a particular problem if the partnership is experiencing cash flow difficulties. The **fixed capital account** shows the original amounts that the individual partners have contributed and is only amended if a partner introduces or withdraws substantial amounts, this could be cash or assets. This usually only takes place by agreement with the other partners. It is possible with the dissolution (ending) of a partnership for a partner to have a debit balance in the capital account, this will be dealt with in a later topic.

The main advantages of keeping fixed capital accounts is that it is easy to determine the current investment position of any partner and can be easily used to calculate interest on capital.

Debit	Credit
Capital withdrawn (cash/other assets)	Bal b/d (opening capital balance)
Intangible assets (goodwill) (written off)	Capital introduced (cash/other assets)
Bal c/d (closing capital balance)	Intangible assets (goodwill) (created)

Fig. 3.1 *Contents of a fixed capital account*

Intangible assets (goodwill) represent the reputation, client base and success of the partnership thus far and rewards the existing partners in the old profit sharing ratio. It is an intangible asset so will normally be amortised (written off) from the balance sheet in the new profit sharing ratio. It can also be the difference between the worth of the partnership, the net assets and how much it could be sold for.

Current accounts

A **current account** is used for the partners to record their share of profits or losses, salaries, total drawings and any interest on drawings or capital. The opening balance could either be a debit or a credit. A debit balance signifies that a partner has withdrawn more money than they are entitled to and, therefore, are in debt to the firm, and a credit balance that they have increased the level of their current investment in the partnership. A close eye should be kept on current accounts as it is important for cash flow purposes that the partners do not withdraw too much as then additional overdrafts and loans which incur interest could be needed.

The main advantage of then keeping separate fluctuating current accounts is that this makes it immediately apparent if any partner is taking more in drawings they are making in total appropriation of profits, that is if they are eroding their personal capital position.

Importance of current accounts

Current accounts are a useful part of partnership accounts as for the benefit of all partners involved an accurate record must be kept of drawings made, interest on capital or drawings, partnership salaries and appropriated profits and losses. Remember that major changes in actual capital movements are kept separately as far as we are concerned for the examination in a fixed capital account. If we were to merge the two accounts it would make it more difficult to calculate interest on capital and also recognise when a partner is continually drawing out more than they should be and depleting their capital injection. Capital and current

Key terms

Fixed capital accounts: the amount of capital introduced or withdrawn by each partner is recorded in a separate account and does not alter unless agreed by the partnership.

Intangible assets (goodwill): reflects the reputation built up by a partnership, this is an intangible asset and there are several different approaches to valuing it but it is essentially a reflection of the success of the partnership. This could be based on previous profits for example. It could also represent the difference between the net assets of the partnership and the amount it could be sold for.

Current account: this records all the partners' drawings, interest on drawings, interest on capital, partnership salaries and shares of residual profit or loss.

AQA Examiner's tip

The opening balance on the capital account is always credit, think CC, Credit Capital, to remember this.

AQA Examiner's tip

When intangible assets (goodwill) are written off it may be helpful to think of it as being 'destroyed', DD, Debit Destroyed intangible assets (goodwill).

AQA Examiner's tip

To help you remember the layout for a current account remember LID (loss, interest on drawings, drawings) and SIP (salaries, interest on capital and profit). Interest on drawings is entered on the same side as drawings.

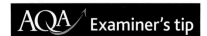

Prepare current accounts in the columnar form, with all partners as shown in this chapter. It will save you time in the exam.

Activity

3 What are the advantages of maintaining separate current and capital accounts for Bonnie and Lucinda?

Link

Look back at trading and profit and loss accounts for sole traders which you studied as part of AS Unit 1. Partnership final accounts are very similar to those of a sole trader.

accounts both represent the amounts owed to the partners. Current accounts take the short-term view whereas capital accounts are long-term and are only affected by permanent change.

Illustration

Example of a current account

Dr	Current Account					Cr
	B	L		B	L	
Bal b/d	5,500		Bal b/d		12,200	
Interest on drawings	800	900	Salaries	15,000	15,000	
Drawings	18,500	24,400	Interest on capital	1,000	800	
			Profit	6,000	6,000	
Bal c/d		8,700	Bal c/d	2,800		
	24,800	34,000		24,800	34,000	
Bal b/d	2,800		Bal b/d		8,700	

Fig. 3.2 *An example of a current account for the two partners Bonnie and Lucinda*

The balances brought down at the start reveal that Bonnie owes the partnership £5,500 whilst the partnership owes Lucinda £12,200. Bonnie continues to withdraw more than she is entitled to as shown by the closing balance brought down which is a debit balance. Lucinda has not made drawings in excess of the salary and interest on capital built up and remains with a credit balance of £8,700.

Appropriation accounts

Income statements (trading and profit and loss accounts) are exactly the same for partnerships as they are for a sole trader. The only difference comes after the profit for the year (net profit) has been calculated. An appropriation account is now added on to show where the net profit is distributed, that is how much profit or loss each partner receives and why. There are just four possible entries that may occur, interest on drawings, interest on capital, salaries and the share of any profits/losses each partner receives. You are making these adjustments from the point of view of the partnership as a whole and not for the individual partner. For example, interest on drawings reduces the individual partner's current account balance but increases the profit for the year (net profit) for the partnership. This is a way of penalising a partner who is withdrawing significant amounts. If there is less cash in the partnership then an overdraft or loan may be needed which would incur interest and hence reduce profits. The best source of finance for any business is from profit rather than external sources which have interest rates and arrangement fees attached.

A profit is credited to the partner's current account and a loss is debited to the partner's current account. You must ensure that you calculate interest on drawings and interest on capital separately for each partner and show them separately as shown in the illustration. You will either be given the interest on capital or interest on drawings figures or asked to calculate them using whatever percentage is given.

The examination question will normally tell you the profit sharing ratio. If it does not you should assume that the profits or losses are shared equally according to the Partnership Act 1890.

Illustration

Sharing profits

Harold, Moheber and Jane share their profits 3:2:1 respectively, this means that Harold receives the highest amount of profit. If the profit after adjusting for interest on drawings, interest on capital and salaries was £60,000 then divide £60,000 by 6 (3+2+1) and then multiply by 3 for Harold so £30,000, 2 for Moheber £20,000 and 1 for Jane £10,000. Add the individual partners' share of the profits together to check that they match the overall profit after appropriation.

Illustration

Income statement (profit and loss appropriation account)

Bonnie and Lucinda share their profits and losses equally as shown in the illustration of the current account. You can trace the entries from the current account onto the income statement (profit and loss appropriation account). The **profit and loss appropriation account** is constructed prior to the current accounts.

Key term

Profit and loss appropriation account: this account records the distribution of profits among partners based on any agreement made by the partners. Where there is no agreement the terms of the Partnership Act 1890 should be applied. The account includes interest on drawings, interest on capital, partnership salaries and the share of the residual profit or loss.

Income statement (profit and loss appropriation account) for Bonnie and Lucinda for the year ended 31 March 2008

		£	£
Net profit			42,100
Add	Interest charged on drawings – Bonnie	800	
	– Lucinda	900	1,700
			43,800
Less	Salaries – Bonnie	15,000	
	– Lucinda	15,000	(30,000)
Less	Interest on capital – Bonnie	1,000	
	– Lucinda	800	(1,800)
			12,000
	Share of remaining profits		
	– Bonnie		6,000
	– Lucinda		6,000
			12,000

Fig. 3.3 *Income statement (profit and loss appropriation account)*

In this topic you will have learnt:

- how partners share their profits or losses
- the contents of a partnership agreement and the implications of the Partnership Act 1890 if there is no agreement
- the purpose and content of fixed capital and current accounts
- how to prepare a current account
- how to prepare a income statement (profit and loss appropriation account).

1   Explain why a successful sole trader may wish to enter into a partnership.

2   Sam and Jack were good friends and did not draw up a deed of partnership when they launched their gardening partnership. Outline the consequences of their decision.

3   George, Joseph and Stuart are in partnership together and have provided the following information for the year ended 31 December 2008:

	George £	Joseph £	Stuart £
Drawings	4,000	3,800	3,000
Interest on drawings	630	585	525
Capital	22,000	33,500	19,500
Partnership salaries	0	10,000	5,000
Opening balances of current accounts	600 credit	400 debit	350 debit
Share of profit	8,000	8,000	8,000

Interest is allowed on partners' capitals at the rate of 6% per annum.

Required

Prepare the partnership current accounts at 31 December 2008.

4   Mitesh, Sailesh and Kishen own a sports equipment shop. They share profits and losses in the ratios of 2:2:1 respectively and have provided you with the following information for the year ended 30 September 2008.

	Mitesh £	Sailesh £	Kishen £
Capital	78,000	42,000	95,500
Partnership salaries	10,000	0	15,000
Drawings	4,000	2,500	3,300

There is no interest on drawings. Interest on capital is to be allowed at 8%. The profit for the year (net profit) was £62,800.

Required

Prepare a income statement (profit and loss appropriation account) for the year ended 30 September 2008.

5   AQA Summer 2005

On 1 March 2004, Tom entered into partnership with his friend Eliza and a partnership agreement was drawn up. It provided that:

fixed capital accounts are to be maintained at: Tom £70,000 and Eliza £25,000; in addition, partnership current accounts are to be maintained.

It further provided that:

■ Profits and losses are to be shared in the ratio of 2:1 respectively.

■ Eliza is to be credited with a partnership salary of £8,000 per annum.

■ Partners are to be credited with interest on their capital accounts at the rate of 6% per annum.

■ Interest is to be charged on partners' drawings.

The net profit for the year ended 28 February 2005 was £11,467.

Information supplied for the year ended 28 February 2005

	Tom £	Eliza £
Partners' drawings for the year were	21,460	18,500
Interest charged on drawings was	637	420

Examiner's tip

Make sure you show each partner's interest on capital or drawings or salaries as separate items and not as a total figure.

Required

(a)   Prepare an income statement (profit and loss appropriation account) for the year ended 28 February 2005.

(b)   Prepare partnership current accounts at 28 February 2005.

(c)   Explain briefly what the closing balances on the partners' current accounts indicate.

Topic 2

Preparing the final accounts of partnerships: more complex profit sharing arrangements

In this topic you will learn how to:

■ prepare end of year financial statements (final accounts), including the balance sheet of partnerships

■ prepare income statements (profit and loss appropriation accounts) and current accounts where profit sharing arrangements have changed during the course of the year.

■ Balance sheets of a partnership

The balance sheet of a partnership is very similar in many respects to a balance sheet of a sole trader with sections for non-current assets (fixed assets), current assets, current liabilities and non-current (long-term) liabilities. The difference comes at the end with the Financed by section, which shows where the capital has come from to fund the partnership. This is made up of both the fixed capital and the current accounts of all the partners. It is common practice to show the final capital account balance and then the breakdown of the current accounts. It is then clear how much each partner has invested or withdrawn from the partnership, how much profit they have received and so on. A debit balance on a current account is shown as a negative with brackets on a balance sheet.

A balance sheet extract for a partnership

Balance sheet (extract) for Neelum and Lloyd at 31 December 2008

	£	£	£
Financed by:			
Capital accounts			
Neelum		150,000	
Lloyd		225,000	
			375,000
Current accounts	Neelum	Lloyd	
Opening balance	2,200	(800)	
Add: salary	13,500	15,000	
Interest on capital	7,500	11,250	
Share of profit	20,000	20,000	
	43,200	45,450	
Less: drawings	25,300	40,000	
Interest on drawings	8,800	9,350	
	9,100	(3,900)	
			5,200
			380,200

Fig. 3.4 *Balance sheet extract for a partnership*

The closing balances on the current accounts are a credit for Neelum of £9,100 and a debit for Lloyd of £3,900. This means that Lloyd owes the partnership £3,900 and the partnership owes Neelum £9,100. Their closing balances are netted off to arrive at £5,200 which is then added to their closing capital accounts of £375,000 to show the balancing figure of £380,200.

Changes in partnership agreements

There will be times when a partner wishes to introduce more capital or withdraw some. It might be agreed that the current profit sharing ratio is not now a fair reflection of the amount of risk or work being undertaken by each partner and that it needs changing. The essential point to remember is to produce a profit and loss appropriation account for the time period before the change and then another one for the following period. So, if a partner introduced capital six months into the financial year you would need to complete an appropriation account with the interest on capital for his original amount of capital and then another one for the second six months which has the interest calculated on the new amount of capital. Examination questions could involve one partner introducing more capital and the other withdrawing some so you essentially have four different amounts of interest on capital to calculate. Questions could also involve changes in the partners' profit sharing ratio to reflect any changes in working practices or investment positions.

Illustration

Example of a change in capital

Jeff, Simon and Beth are partners in the Pony Shack which sells horse equipment. Their accounting period is for 12 months from 1 January. They have agreed that interest on capital is 5%. Jeff's capital balance was £200,000 throughout the year. Simon's capital balance was £200,000 until 1 July when he increased it to £340,000. Beth's capital balance was £300,000 until she reduced it by £116,000 on 1 July. The net profit for the year was £68,000 and is accrued equally each month. They share profits and losses equally.

You need to calculate 2 separate interest on capital figures for both Simon and Beth as they have different amounts of capital during the year.

Simon has 200,000 × 5% = 10,000 then divide by 2 as it is for half a year = £5,000.

Then, 340,000 × 5% = 17,000 divide by 2 = £8,500.

Activity

6 Show how Beth's interest on capital has been calculated.

Income statement (profit and loss appropriation account) for Jeff, Simon and Beth for the year ended 31 December 2008

		£	£
Profit for the year			68,000
Less	Interest on capital – Jeff	10,000	
	– Simon	13,500	
	– Beth	12,100	
			35,600
			32,400
	Share of remaining profits		
	– Jeff		10,800
	–Simon		10,800
	– Beth		10,800
			32,400

Fig. 3.5 *Income statement (profit and loss appropriation account) showing a change in capital*

Illustration

Changes in a partnership agreement

The following income statement (profit and loss appropriation account) shows how a change of partnership agreement part way through the year should be shown. Originally the partners split the profits and losses equally but on 1 June they decide to share profits 3:2 and to have interest on capital. It is assumed that the profit of £80,000 has accrued evenly throughout the year. The profit for the year for the first six months is £40,000. For the second six months the interest on capital is subtracted to leave £38,200. This is then shared between the partners by dividing £38,200 by 5 and then multiplying by 3 for Spencer which is £22,920 and by 2 for Olivia which is £15,280.

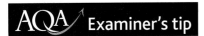
In this topic you will have learnt:

- how to complete a set of financial statements (final accounts) for a partnership

- how to prepare income statements (profit and loss appropriation accounts) and current accounts where there have been changes during the year such as profit sharing or capital balances.

Income statement (profit and loss appropriation account) for Spencer and Olivia for the year ended 31 December 2008

		£	£
Profit for the year – first 6 months			40,000
Share of profits	– Spencer	20,000	
	– Olivia	20,000	
			40,000
Profit for the year – second 6 months			40,000
	Interest on capital		
Less	– Spencer	1,000	
	– Olivia	800	
			1,800
			38,200
	Share of remaining profits		
	– Spencer		22,920
	– Olivia		15,280
			38,200

Fig. 3.6 *Income statement (profit and loss appropriation account) showing a change in partnership agreement*

 Examination-style questions

1   AQA January 2004

Jackie Hall owns and runs a bookshop. She employs her brother Bryan as the buyer for the shop and he is very good at his job. Jackie is considering offering Bryan a partnership starting on 1 April 2004. As the business is very successful she will not require him to contribute any capital.

Required

Discuss whether or not Jackie should enter into a partnership.

2   Luke and Charlie are partners in a sauna installation business and have the following partnership agreement:

- ■ partnership salaries are Luke £12,000 and Charlie £10,000 per annum
- ■ interest on capital 10% per annum
- ■ profits and losses to be shared equally.

Capital and current account balances at 31 May 2008

	Luke £	Charlie £
Capital account	48,000	20,000
Current account	3,500 credit	1,500 debit

The following information was available for the year ending 31 May 2008, after the preparation of the income statement (trading and profit and loss account):

	£
Drawings – Luke	12,000
Drawings – Charlie	14,000
Net profit	72,000
Premises at cost	75,000
Vans at cost	32,000
Bank	8,100
Cash	2,500
Trade receivables (trade debtors)	8,600
Trade payables (creditors)	3,100
Provision for depreciation for vans	8,000

Required

(a)   A income statement (profit and loss appropriation account) for the year ended 31 May 2008.

(b)   A balance sheet at 31 May 2008.

3   Lauren and Emmie are in partnership and start on 1 January 2008 with no partnership agreement. Lauren is then advised by her accountant to draw up a partnership agreement and on 1 July 2008 it is agreed that:

■   profits will be shared 2:1 respectively
■   interest on capital accounts will be 10% per annum
■   interest will be charged on drawings
■   partnership salaries will be introduced.

Profit for 2008 was £68,000 accrued evenly.

	Lauren £	Emmie £
Capital accounts 1 January 2008	30,000	20,000
Current accounts 1 January 2008	1,300 credit	3,200 debit
Drawings for the year	14,200	12,750
Partnership salaries	10,000	8,000
Interest on drawings	850	700

Required

(a)   Prepare the income statement (profit and loss appropriation account) for the year ended 31 December 2008.

(b)   Prepare the partners' current accounts for the year ended 31 December 2008.

4   Stephen, James and Will are in partnership sharing profits and losses in the ratio 2:2:1 respectively. During the year ended 30 November 2008 the net profit was £48,400.

The following information is provided at 30 November 2008:

	Stephen £	James £	Will £
Capital accounts 1 December 2007	50,000	60,000	30,000
Current accounts 1 December 2007	600 credit	400 debit	1,000 credit
Drawings for the year	2,000	1,800	500
Partnership salaries	0	3,000	2,000

Interest is charged on drawings at a rate of 8% per annum and interest allowed on capital of 6% per annum. The partners agreed that James should withdraw £10,000 from his capital and that Will should introduce the same amount on 1 June 2008.

Required

(a)   Prepare the income statement (profit and loss appropriation account) for the year ended 30 November 2008.

(b)   Prepare the partners' capital and current accounts for the year ended 30 November 2008.

4 Partnership and changes in partners

In this chapter we build on chapter 3 and consider the accounting approaches needed in order to record the retirement and/or admission of a partner. We also look at what happens when a partnership is dissolved. The **retirement of a partner** could be followed by the admission of a new partner. When a partner retires we need to calculate how much the retiring partner is due to receive and how best this can be funded. If a new partner joins we need to ensure that our assets are appropriately valued. Intangible assets (goodwill) need to be considered in both situations. When a partnership comes to an end, the reality of having unlimited liability can become an issue with some partners having to cover the shortfall of others who may not have the required capital to cover their share of losses. It is important to take a logical approach to all types of partnership question and read carefully what the key changes are, making note of the date when any changes occurred and then act accordingly.

Topic 1 Retirement of a partner

In this topic you will learn how to:

- calculate a revaluation surplus or deficit based on changes in asset values perhaps upon the retirement of a partner

- divide a revaluation surplus or deficit among the partners

- explain the term 'intangible assets' (goodwill) and why it is not normally recorded in accounting records

- calculate the adjustment necessary to partners' capital balances as a result of valuing intangible assets (goodwill) upon the retirement of a partner

- record the return of capital to a retiring partner by implementing various options including transfer of funds to a loan account, payment in cash or by the transfer of another asset

A limited company has its own separate legal entity and continues independently of its shareholders; with a partnership, when one partner die, or leaves a partnership then a new partnership is formed.

Case study

Walker, Scott and Cavendish

Walker, Scott and Cavendish are a successful partnership in Manchester who are estate agents dealing exclusively with the luxury end of the market. In addition to selling houses and apartments they also have a rental division which is particularly in demand from city workers who want the convenience of living in the city centre with all it has to offer. Cavendish has decided that he would now like to spend time with his family and would like to retire from the fast-paced life of property.

Stages needed when a partner retires

When a partner retires it is important to calculate how much their share of the partnership is worth. The other partners can then decide how best to finance this share, for example the retiring partner could transfer the amount due to a loan account, a loan from the bank could be used, or the decision whether to bring a new partner in who can replace the retiring one and bring in capital themselves can be made.

1 We need to begin with the capital from the most recent balance sheet.

2 Add to this any revaluation surplus or deduct deficit due to the partner.

- prepare the balance sheet of the new partnership after the retirement of a partner

- evaluate the options open to a partnership in returning the capital of a retiring partner.

3 Make **adjustments for intangible assets (goodwill)**.

4 Add the latest current account balance if in credit or deduct if it is a debit.

5 Decide how to pay the retiring partner the amount due.

Revaluation and intangible assets (goodwill)

These two processes are linked together as we will see in the following illustration. The **revaluation account** records the change in value of assets such as premises or inventory (stock). Premises will usually have increased in value whereas other assets such as inventory (stock) may have fallen in value. Intangible assets (goodwill) are essentially paid by the new partner but shared by the existing partners if they carry on, to gain access to future profits that will hopefully be generated by the partnership. Intangible assets (goodwill) reflect the client base or profits which has been built up over the partnership. It is only fair to reward a retiring partner with their share of having established and developed a successful partnership. Goodwill is intangible which means it has no physical substance and since it is largely based on reputation, the popularity of the product or service it could be lost very quickly. For this reason it is often considered good practice to write it off, in other words remove it from the balance sheet. If intangible assets (goodwill) are to remain on the books it appears as an asset on the balance sheet. You create goodwill in the old partnership profit sharing ratio and write it off it in the new partnership profit sharing ratio.

Illustration

Retirement of a partner

Walker, Scott and Cavendish, share profits and losses in the ratio 2:2:1. They provide the following information:

Balance sheet for Walker, Scott and Cavendish at 30 April 2008

	£	£
Non-current (fixed) assets		85,000
Current assets	60,000	
Current liabilities	22,500	37,500
		122,500
Capital accounts – Walker		50,000
– Scott		25,000
– Cavendish		47,500
		122,500

Fig. 4.1 *Summary balance sheet*

Cavendish has decided to retire on 30 April 2008.

The partners have agreed that:

- fixed assets be valued at £100,000

- intangible assets (goodwill) be valued at £40,000 and then be written off

- from 1 May 2008 profits and losses will be shared equally.

Firstly, we need to prepare a revaluation account:

Dr		Revaluation Account		Cr
Inventory (stock)	2,000	Non-current (fixed) assets	15,000	
Capital a/c – W	21,200	Intangible assets (goodwill)	40,000	
– S	21,200			
– C	10,600			
	55,000		55,000	

Fig. 4.2 *Revaluation account*

The non-current (fixed) assets entry of £15,000 is how much the fixed assets have increased in value by. Inventory (stock) has fallen in value by £2,000 perhaps it has deteriorated or is less popular now. £55,000 is then split between the partners in the old profit sharing ratio. The double entry is to debit the non-current (fixed) assets account by £15,000 and credit the revaluation account with £15,000.

Dr		Intangible Assets (Goodwill) Account		Cr
Revaluation	40,000	Capital – W	20,000	
		– C	20,000	
	40,000		40,000	

Fig. 4.3 *Intangible assets (goodwill) account*

To write off the intangible assets (goodwill) account we split the amount between the remaining partners in the new profit sharing amount.

We are now ready to enter these amounts in the capital accounts. As with current accounts it is much easier for both you and the examiner if you use the layout shown below rather than individual accounts for each partner.

Dr				Current Account				Cr
	W	S	C		W	S	C
Intangible assets (goodwill)	20,000	20,000	–	Bal b/d	50,000	25,000	47,500
Loan			58,100	Revaluation	21,200	21,200	10,600
Bal c/d	51,200	26,200					
	71,200	46,200	58,100		71,200	46,200	58,100
				Bal b/d	51,200	26,200	

Fig. 4.4 *Capital accounts*

As you can see, instead of Cavendish having a closing capital account balance he has a loan which is how much the partnership owes him for his share in the partnership. The remaining partners need to decide how best to deal with paying this amount to him.

The new balance sheet will look like this:

Balance sheet for Walker and Scott at 30 April 2008

	£	£
Non-current (fixed) assets		100,000
Current assets	58,000	
Current liabilities	22,500	35,500
		135,500
Capital accounts – Walker		51,200
– Scott		26,200
Loan – Cavendish		58,100
		135,500

Fig. 4.5 *Balance sheet after retirement*

How to settle liability owing to the retiring partner

There are several ways that this can be done:

1 Introduce a new partner and use the capital they introduce to pay off the retiring partner. If there will be a gap in skills or knowledge or finance or too much work for the remaining partners then the admission of a new partner should be considered.

2 Bank overdraft. If a large enough overdraft can be secured this can be a flexible way of paying the partner as it can be easily repaid once enough cash is in the business and finance costs (interest) are only charged on the amount outstanding. If we know we are soon to receive a substantial amount in revenue (sales) or income then this could be a good idea.

3 Bank loan. This could be used over a longer time period and if a large sum is needed. It will affect our monthly cash flow as usually finance costs (interest) and part of the capital will be repaid each month. Budgeting will be easier as we know the exact amount each month.

4 Loan from retiring partner. This may have a cheaper interest rate than the loan or overdraft but it could mean that the retiring partner still wishes to maintain some control and have a say over the partnership and its decisions.

Activity

1 Consider the advantages and disadvantages of the different ways in which Cavendish can be repaid his investment.

In this topic you will have learnt:

- how to record the revaluation of tangible assets on the retirement of a partner

- why intangible assets (goodwill) are not normally recorded in the accounting system and how an adjustment for goodwill should be made in the partners' capital accounts

- how to redraft the balance sheet immediately after the retirement of a partner

- how the remaining partners can discharge any liability to the retiring partner and the benefits and drawbacks of the options.

1   Lewis, Eric and Katie are in partnership, sharing profits and losses in the ratio 3:2:1. They provide the following information:

Balance sheet for Lewis, Eric and Katie at 30 September 2008

	£	£
Non-current (fixed) assets		120,000
Other current assets	36,000	
Bank	2,000	
Current liabilities	(22,000)	16,000
		136,000
Capital accounts – Lewis		82,000
– Eric		30,000
– Katie		24,000
		136,000

Eric has decided to retire on 30 September 2008.

The partners have agreed that:

■   non-current (fixed) assets be valued at £135,000

■   current assets (excluding bank) valued at £33,000

■   intangible assets (goodwill) be valued at £48,000 and then be written off.

Lewis and Katie will continue in partnership, sharing profits and losses equally. Eric's share will initially be placed in a loan account.

Required

(a)   Prepare the three partners' capital accounts at 30 September 2008, showing the effects of Eric's retirement.

(b)   Prepare a balance sheet at 30 September 2008, following Eric's retirement.

2   AQA Summer 2002

Mary, Nerine and Oliver are in partnership sharing profits and losses in the ratio 3:2:1 respectively. Nerine retired from the partnership on 30 April 2002.

Mary and Oliver have continued in partnership after Nerine's retirement. They share profits and losses equally.

The summarised partnership balance sheet as at 30 April 2002 was as follows:

	£
Non-current (fixed) assets	120,000
Net current assets	25,000
	145,000
Capital accounts – Mary	75,000
– Nerine	40,000
– Oliver	30,000
	145,000

The following values have been agreed by the partners as at 30 April 2002 prior to Nerine's retirement from the partnership.

	£
Non-current (fixed) assets	142,000
Net current assets	23,000
Intangible assets (goodwill)	28,000

It has been agreed that intangible assets (goodwill) will not appear in the books of the partnership. As a temporary measure any settlement due to Nerine will be treated as a loan to the new partnership.

Required

(a) Calculate the amount due to Nerine on her retirement.

(b) Evaluate one method of settling the debt owed to Nerine on her retirement, other than borrowing from a bank.

3 AQA January 2006

Mei, Janet and Michael have been in partnership for a number of years, sharing profits and losses in the ratio 3:2:1 respectively.

The summarised partnership balance sheet at 30 September 2005 is shown below:

	£	£
Non-current (fixed) assets		60,000
Bank	1,000	
Other current assets	28,000	
	29,000	
Current liabilities	(24,000)	5,000
		65,000
Capital accounts: Mei		40,000
Janet		20,000
Michael		5,000
		65,000

Janet retired from the partnership at close of business on 30 September 2005. Mei and Michael continued in partnership; they shared profits in the ratio 2:1 respectively. The three partners agreed that the following asset valuations applied at 30 September 2005.

	£
Non-current (fixed) assets	130,000
Intangible assets (goodwill)	75,000
Current assets (excluding bank)	27,000

It was further agreed that intangible assets (goodwill) would not appear in the books of the account. Mei and Michael were unsure how any debt owed to Janet should be settled. In the short term, the amount was transferred to a temporary loan account.

Mei and Michael are considering three alternative methods of funding the amount owed to Janet.

These are:

i   to borrow sufficient funds from a bank in the form of a long-term loan, repayable in equal monthly instalments over ten years at 8% interest per annum

ii   to use overdraft facilities (the bank has agreed to this if required)

iii to leave the amount due in Janet's loan account, repayable over ten years in equal half-yearly instalments at 7% interest per annum.

Required

(a)   Prepare the three partners' capital accounts at 30 September 2005, showing the effects of Janet's retirement.

(b)   Advise Mei and Michael how the debt to Janet should be settled.

Topic 2   Admission of a partner

In this topic you will learn how to:

- calculate and share a revaluation of assets prior to the admission of a partner

- calculate and make entries for a goodwill adjustment in the capital accounts of the partners

- record the capital introduced by an incoming partner

- record entries to alter the relative balances of partners' capital accounts where individual partners pay in, or take out, funds

- prepare the balance sheet after the admission of the new partner.

In this topic we will be examining the accounting entries needed for the admission of a partner. We may need a new partner because an existing one has retired, left or because we require additional capital. It could also be that we have a gap in our skills or knowledge and require the expertise of a new partner. Whatever the reason it is essential that we consider the intangible assets (goodwill) that have already been built up in the current partnership, revalue the tangible assets and reward the existing partners accordingly.

Revaluation

If a revaluation takes place which increases the value of the asset, which is usually the case with premises, then we:

- **Debit** revaluation account
- **Credit** each partner in their profit sharing ratio prior to the new partner.

If the asset has fallen in value, as could be the case with inventory (stock), then we should:

- **Debit** each partner in their profit sharing ratio prior to the new partner
- **Credit** revaluation account.

Illustration

Admitting a new partner and revaluation

Walker and Scott have decided to admit Rahman into their partnership as they have found it difficult to cope since the retirement of Cavendish. They currently share profits and losses equally. At 31 December 2008, their assets had the following values:

	£
Non-current (fixed) assets	
Premises	200,000
Fixtures and fittings	64,000
Motor vehicles	36,000
	300,000

Fig. 4.6 *Non-current (fixed) assets*

Rahman is admitted as a partner on 1 January 2009 when the assets were revalued as follows:

	£
Non-current (fixed) assets	
Premises	300,000
Fixtures and fittings	50,000
Motor vehicles	24,000
	374,000

Fig. 4.7 *Revaluation of assets*

Dr		Revaluation Account		Cr
	£			£
Fixtures and fittings	14,000	Premises		100,000
Motor vehicles	12,000			
Capital – Walker	37,000			
Capital – Scott	37,000			
	100,000			100,000

Fig. 4.8 *Revalued non-current (fixed) assets*

Walker and Scott's capital accounts will both be credited with £37,000 to reflect the overall increase in assets of £74,000 which is the increase in premises of £100,000 less the fall in value of the fixtures and fittings and motor vehicles of £26,000.

Treatment of intangible assets (goodwill)

Goodwill is an intangible asset which is often calculated when a partner joins or leaves the partnership to reflect the success so far of the partnership. It is considered good accounting practice to write off intangible assets (goodwill) immediately as shown here:

1 Not to remain in books

The first stage is as above:

- ■ **Debit** intangible assets (goodwill) account
- ■ **Credit** existing partners' capital accounts in old profit sharing ratio.

We then need to remove the goodwill:

- ■ **Debit** all partners' capital accounts in new profit sharing ratio
- ■ **Credit** goodwill account.

To create intangible assets (goodwill) we credit in old ratio and to destroy (write off) intangible assets (goodwill) we debit in the new ratio.

2 To remain in books

- ■ **Debit** intangible assets (goodwill) account
- ■ **Credit** existing partners' capital accounts in old profit sharing ratio.

If goodwill remains then it is shown on the balance sheet in the fixed assets section.

■ Illustration

Admitting a new partner and goodwill

Brian and Chris are partners in a firm and share profits equally. Their capital account balances are £75,000 and £50,000 respectively. On 1 January 2009 they admit Jerry as a partner when the profit or loss sharing ratio will be Brian $\frac{2}{5}$, Chris $\frac{2}{5}$ and Jerry $\frac{1}{5}$. Intangible assets (goodwill) are valued at £15,000 and is to be written off. Jerry paid £45,000 into the firm's bank account and brings in a van worth £5,000 as capital.

Table 1 *Share of intangible assets (goodwill)*

	First stage Old partner sharing Create goodwill = credit	Second stage New partner sharing Destroy goodwill = debit
Brian	$\frac{1}{2}$ = £7,500	$\frac{2}{5}$ = £6,000
Chris	$\frac{1}{2}$ = £7,500	$\frac{2}{5}$ = £6,000
Jerry	-	$\frac{1}{5}$ = £3,000

We can now enter these amounts into the capital accounts.

Dr				Capital Account			Cr
	B	C	J		B	C	J
Intangible assets (goodwill)	6,000	6,000	3,000	Bal b/d	75,000	50,000	
				Bank			45,000
				Van			5,000
Bal c/d	76,500	51,500	47,000	Goodwill	7,500	7,500	
	82,500	57,500	50,000		82,500	57,500	50,000
				Bal b/d	76,500	51,500	47,000

Fig. 4.9 *Capital accounts*

The money and van which Jerry introduces will be debited to the bank and van accounts and credited to the capital account. The overall effect of Jerry joining the partnership is that Brian and Chris now have increased capital account balances and Jerry's balance is less than the amount he has contributed. He has in effect, bought his way into the partnership.

	£	£
Capital accounts – Brian		76,500
– Chris		51,500
– Jerry		47,000
		175,000

Fig. 4.10 *Balance sheet extract to show new capital account balances*

Changes needed in the final accounts to reflect the introduction of a new partner

As we saw in the previous topic, if there is a change to the partnership agreement about sharing profits or losses or investment revenue (interest) on capital etc. during the year the appropriation account needs splitting into two sections to show this. In the same way, if a new partner is introduced during the year then we need to draw up an income statement (profit and loss appropriation account) prior to the new partner joining and then for when the period after they have joined. On the balance sheet we must adjust for any cash or fixed assets they have introduced and also show their new capital account balance which may well be less than they introduced if intangible assets (goodwill) were introduced and then written off.

In this topic you will have learnt:

- why a new partner may be introduced and the need to ensure existing partners are suitably rewarded for their previous efforts
- how to make adjustments for intangible assets (goodwill)
- how to record the capital introduced by the new partner
- how to appropriate profits in a year when a new partner has been introduced part way through
- how to redraft a partnership balance sheet immediately after the admission of a partner.

Activity

2 In pairs, discuss the potential advantages and disadvantages to admitting a new partner into a partnership which has been in existence for 10 years.

AQA Examination-style questions

1   Salmon and Tennant share profits 2:1 respectively. They admit Johnson as a partner on 1 July 2008, who will contribute £40,000 cash as capital.

Balance sheet for Salmon and Tennant at 30 June 2008

	£	£
Non-current (fixed) assets		
Premises		170,000
Motor vehicles		85,000
		255,000
Current assets		
Inventory (stock)	12,000	
Bank	3,500	
		15,500
		270,500
Capital accounts – Salmon		150,000
– Tennant		120,500
		270,500

The partners decide to revalue their assets as follows:

	£
Premises	220,000
Motor vehicles	70,000
Inventory (stock)	10,000

Required

(a)   Prepare capital accounts for the three partners after the revaluation takes place.

(b)   Prepare the balance sheet after Johnson has joined the partnership at 1 July 2008.

2   AQA Summer 2007

Daniel and Freda commenced business in partnership on 1 January 2005. They had no partnership agreement and decided not to keep proper books of account.

Capital introduced by each partner on 1 January 2005 was as follows:

Daniel £20,000 and Freda £30,000.

The following information is given at 31 December 2005, at the end of the first year of trading.

	£
Premises	40,000
Vehicle	3,750
Office equipment	6,000
Inventory (stock)	2,400
Trade receivables (debtors)	150
Trade payables (creditors)	3,250
Cash at bank	10,950

Daniel had withdrawn £17,000 and Freda had withdrawn £23,000 for personal use during the year.

Required

(a) Calculate the partnership profit or loss for the year ended 31 December 2005. An income statement (profit and loss account) is not required.

During the early part of 2006, the partners thought that the business was doing so well that the time had come to expand. In order to finance the expansion, Helen was admitted as a partner with effect from 1 July 2006. The partners drew up a written agreement to take effect from 1 July 2006. The agreement provided that:

i Helen be credited with a partnership salary of £5,000 per annum

ii partners be credited with interest on capital at 6% per annum

iii residual profits and losses be shared in the ratios Daniel $\frac{1}{2}$; Freda $\frac{1}{3}$; Helen $\frac{1}{6}$

iv partners be charged finance costs (interest) on drawings.

The agreement further provided that the partners would maintain separate capital and current accounts.

At 30 June 2006, the partnership balance sheet was as follows.

	£	£
Non-current (fixed) assets		
Premises		40,000
Vehicle		3,125
Office equipment		5,700
		48,825
Current liabilities		
Inventory (stock)	3,200	
Trade receivables (trade debtors)	1,985	
Bank	3,170	
	8,355	
Current liabilities		
Trade payables (trade creditors)	(4,180)	4,175
		53,000
Capital accounts – Daniel		25,000
– Freda		28,000
		53,000

When Helen was admitted to the partnership, it was agreed that certain assets would be valued at the following amounts.

	£
Non-current (fixed) assets	100,000
Inventory (stock)	2,600
Trade receivables (debtors)	1,410
Intangible assets (goodwill)	60,000

It was further agreed that the intangible assets (goodwill) would not appear in the business books of account.

Helen agreed to introduce £50,000 cash as capital.

Required

(b)   Prepare the partners' capital accounts as they would appear on 1 July 2006, immediately after Helen was admitted as a partner.

The profit for the year ended 31 December 2006 was £90,000. The profit had accrued evenly throughout the year.

The drawings and finance costs (interest) on drawings for the year for each partner are given below:

	Daniel £	Freda £	Helen £
Drawings	41,000	35,000	12,000
Finance costs (interest) charged on drawings	250	80	160

Required

(c)   Prepare income statement (profit and loss appropriation accounts) for the year ended 31 December 2006.

(d)   Prepare partners' current accounts for the year ended 31 December 2006.

(e)   Evaluate the decision to keep separate capital and current accounts.

Topic 3   Dissolution of a partnership

In this topic you will learn how to:

■ explain the reasons why partnerships dissolve

■ prepare a realisation account recording the disposal of assets for cash, transfer of assets to partners, sale of assets to a company in return for shares and/or debentures, expenses on dissolution, discounts received

■ share the profit or loss on realisation between the partners

■ share the deficiency on a capital account of a partner applying the rule in the case Garner v. Murray

■ prepare the capital accounts of the partner showing the final settlement of the amounts owing to the partners.

■ Key terms

Dissolution: this takes place when a partnership ceases to continue operating. It could be because the partners want this to happen or are forced to because of problems such as lack of cash and/or profit.

Realisation account: used to close the partnership and calculate the profit or loss for the partners once all the assets have been sold or taken over.

■ Reasons for dissolution

Unlike a limited company which can continue in existence regardless of changes in ownership, if anything happens to one of the partners of a partnership then that partnership is dissolved, ceases to exist, and a new one emerges if that is what the remaining partners desire. It could be that a partner wishes to set up independently, is declared bankrupt, dies or wishes to retire.

It is important that the partnership uses its assets to cover any debts in the order of: trade payables (creditors), partners' loan accounts and then finally, if there is money remaining, this will go to the partners' capital accounts. Some of the partners may wish to take over assets themselves, alternatively assets may be sold for cash or taken over by another business.

Stages in dissolution

In order to carry out the process of **dissolution** we need to use a **realisation account**:

Table 2 *Contents of a realisation account*

Debit	Credit
The net book value of the assets to be sold (fixed and current assets)	Proceeds from the sale of the assets
Discounts allowed	Discounts received
Costs of the dissolution	Loss on realisation
Profit on realisation	

When our customers and suppliers hear that our partnership is being dissolved then they may in the customers' case not be so willing to pay us in full and in the suppliers' case be willing to receive less than we originally owed. The discounts allowed are calculated by starting with our trade receivables (debtors) figure and then subtracting what we actually receive from them. The discounts received amount are the trade payables (creditors) from our balance sheet less what we actually pay them. There will either be a profit or loss on realisation, not both.

Follow these 8 stages below:

1 Enter opening balances of the ledger accounts for example, capital accounts, realisation and bank accounts, you have been asked to produce.

2 Enter the fixed asset values and current assets excluding trade receivables (trade debtors). Do not include the bank balance on the debit of realisation account.

3 Debit bank account with what we actually receive from trade receivables (debtors) (not necessarily what they owed us) and credit bank with what we pay trade payables (creditors).

4 Calculate discounts received and discounts allowed and enter in realisation account.

5 Receive cash for assets sold, debit bank and credit realisation account.

6 If a partner takes over assets then, debit their capital account and credit realisation account with the value of the asset.

7 Close down realisation account and post the balances on the realisation account in the partners' capital accounts.

8 Close down capital account and bank account.

Illustration

Dissolution of a partnership

Martha and Jamie have decided to sell their partnership to Heather for £80,000. They had no partnership agreement. The trade receivables (trade debtors) pay them £8,000 and trade payables (trade creditors) are paid £5,000. Costs of the dissolution are £1,800. Their latest summarised balance sheet is below:

Balance sheet for Martha and Jamie at 30 September

	£	£
Non-current (fixed) assets		40,000
Current assets		
Inventory (stock)	22,000	
Trade receivables (trade debtors)	10,000	
Bank	2,000	
	34,000	
Current liabilities		
Trade payables (trade creditors)	6,000	
Net current assets		28,000
		68,000
Capital accounts – Martha		38,000
– Jamie		30,000
		68,000

Fig. 4.11 *Summarised balance sheet*

Dr		Realisation Account		Cr
Non-current (fixed) assets	40,000	Discounts received	1,000
Inventory (stock)	22,000	Bank – Heather	80,000
Discounts allowed	2,000		
Costs of dissolution	1,800		
Capital – Martha	7,600		
Capital – Jamie	7,600		
	81,000		81,000

Fig. 4.12 *Realisation account*

The discounts are calculated by finding the difference between what they were owed and owing and the actual payments which then took place. The profit on dissolution is £15,200 which is split equally between the two partners since they had no partnership agreement. If they did have it would have been split according to the profit sharing ratio.

Dr			Capital Account		Cr
	M	J		M	J
Bank	45,600	37,600	Bal b/d	38,000	30,000
			Profit on realisation	7,600	7,600
	45,600	37,600		45,600	37,600

Fig. 4.13 *Capital account*

The profit from realisation has been entered in each partners' capital accounts and balancing these accounts off will provide us with the amount each partner is entitled to take from the bank account to finally close down the partnership.

Dr		Bank Account	Cr
Bal b/d	2,000	Trade payables (creditors)	5,000
Trade receivables (trade debtors)	8,000	Costs of dissolution	1,800
Heather	80,000	Capital – Martha	45,600
		Capital – Jamie	37,600
	90,000		90,000

Fig. 4.14 *Bank account*

We can tell that we have completed the process correctly because our bank account has no closing balance. The owners of any business are the last to be repaid.

Transfer of assets to partners

A partner may decide to take over some of the assets, perhaps because they want to set up as a sole trader or start a new partnership. If this happens then we:

- **Credit** the realisation account with the agreed value of the asset taken over
- **Debit** the partners' capital accounts with the agreed value of the asset taken over.

Sale of assets to a company

It is possible that a company may wish to take over some of the assets. They could provide cash, ordinary shares or debentures in return. It is important to note that it is what the ordinary shares are WORTH currently that we need to record and not how much their face value is.

Illustration

Company purchasing partnership

Dylan Ltd agrees to a purchase consideration of £250,000 being made up of: £50,000 cash, £65,000 6% debentures and 25,000 ordinary shares of £1 each. We can set up an account for Dylan Ltd which will show us how much the shares are currently worth.

Dr		Dylan Ltd Account		Cr
	£			£
Realisation	250,000	Bank		50,000
		Debentures		65,000
		Ordinary shares		**135,000**
	250,000			250,000

Fig. 4.15 *Account for Dylan Ltd*

This means that the ordinary shares are currently worth =
$$\frac{£135,000}{25,000} = £5.40 \text{ each.}$$

Unless otherwise stated the purchase consideration in terms of shares and debentures from a company is split amongst the partners in the profit sharing ratio. The entries will be on the debit side of the capital accounts and the credit side of the purchasing company account if one has been set up. Any cash received from the company is debited to the bank account.

Activity

 3 How much are the shares worth each if Stalyvegas Ltd offer us a purchase consideration of £300,000 being made up of; £70,000 cash, £57,000 5% debentures and 30,000 ordinary shares of £2 each?

Garner v Murray

If, after joining the current account balances with the capital accounts, and after transfer of profit or loss on realisation to capital accounts, a capital account ends up with a debit balance this means that the partner concerned owes money and that there is a **capital deficiency**. He or she will need to use their personal cash to cover this debit balance, but what if they do not have enough cash to do this? The **Garner v Murray** case ruled that this shortfall must be covered by the other partners in proportion to their last agreed capitals. Therefore, the partner who had most capital invested according to the most recent balance sheet must take on the largest share of the shortfall.

Key terms

Capital deficiency: occurs when a partner has insufficient funds in their account to cover the loss of the dissolution.

Garner v Murray: this case set the precedent that if one partner cannot pay their share of capital deficiency then the other partners must cover the amount according to their most recent capital account ratio.

Illustration

Sharing a short fall

James has a debit balance on his capital account of £600. His partners Fran and Tim must share this according to their last balance sheet capital account balances. Fran had £9,000 and Tim had £6,000 for their capital accounts which means 3:2. So, £600 needs sharing with Fran contributing £360 ($\frac{600}{5} \times 3$) and Tim £240 ($\frac{600}{5} \times 2$).

Dr				Capital Account			Cr
	£	£	£		£	£	£
	J	F	T		J	F	T
Bal b/d	600			Bal b/d		9,000	6,000
Capital – James		360	240	Capital – Fran	360		
Bank		8,640	5,760	Capital – Tim	240		
	600	9,000	6,000		600	9,000	6,000

Fig. 4.16 *Capital account*

Examiner's tip

As with previous partnership questions it is essential to show detailed workings, for example, when adjusting to deal with a partner's debit balance on their capital account after dissolution.

Instead of calculating the balances carried down, the balancing figures represent the amount Fran and Tim will withdraw from the bank account.

In this topic you will have learnt:

- the reasons why partnerships dissolve
- how to record the realisation of assets and the discharge of liabilities
- how to record assets taken over by a partner
- the preparation of a realisation account to show the profit/loss on realisation and its distribution among partners
- the preparation of capital accounts showing entries arising during the realisation process and the final discharge of any liability to a partner
- how to deal with a deficiency on a partner's capital account using Garner v Murray.

AQA Examination-style questions

1   Explain how the Garner v. Murray ruling should be applied.

2   Khan, Patel and Parekh are in partnership. They have agreed to dissolve the partnership. After realising all assets, Parekh is unable to pay the debit balance due to the firm. The remaining balances on the books are as follows:

	£
Cash at bank	90,000
Capital accounts – Khan	72,000
Patel	24,000
Parekh	(6,000)
	90,000

Required
Prepare the capital accounts of the partnership after dealing with the debit balance on Parekh's account.

3   AQA Summer 2005
Tom and Eliza both agreed that their partnership was not the success that they had both hoped that it might have been. They agreed that the partnership be dissolved on 28 February 2005. Profits and losses were shared 2:1.

At 28 February 2005, the partnership had the following assets and liabilities:

	£
Machinery at valuation	36,000
Three vehicles at valuation	28,000
Inventory (stock) of cleaning materials	430
Amounts owing to suppliers of cleaning materials	340
Amounts owed by customers	1,250
Bank balance	1,167

Immediately prior to dissolution, the partners' current account balances were transferred to their capital accounts. The capital account balances then stood at:

Tom £51,319 credit and Eliza £15,188 credit.

The machinery was sold to Pristine Cleaners Ltd for a purchase consideration of £20,000.

The amount was settled by the issue of 12,000 ordinary shares of £1 each in Pristine Cleaners Ltd.

The partners received half of the shares each.

A vehicle with a book value of £12,000 was taken over by Eliza for £9,000.

The other two vehicles were sold for £15,000 cash.

Inventory (stock) of cleaning materials were sold for £380 cash.

Trade payables (trade creditors) were paid in full.

Debtors paid £1,150 in full settlement.

The cost of dissolution amounted to £2,485.

Required

(a)   Calculate the profit or loss on dissolution.

(b)   Prepare partners' capital accounts to show the closing entries.

4   Ruth, Sasha and Theo have now decided to dissolve their partnership. Their balance sheet at 30 April 2008 is:

Balance sheet for Ruth, Sasha and Theo at 30 April 2008

	£	£
Non-current (fixed) assets		
Premises		62,500
Equipment		15,000
Fixtures and fittings		5,000
Delivery vans		10,000
		92,500
Current assets		
Inventory (stock)	7,500	
Trade receivables (trade debtors)	10,000	
	17,500	
Current liabilities		
Trade payables (trade creditors)	5,000	
Bank	9,250	
	14,250	
Net current assets		3,250
		95,750
Capital accounts – Ruth		**40,000**
– Sasha		**30,000**
– Theo		25,750
		95,750

The directors of Mossley Ltd agrees to take over all of the non-current (fixed) assets, except for the delivery vans at a valuation of £100,000. They will pay £70,000 cash, and also issue to the partners 20,000 ordinary shares of £1 each. Ruth and Sasha take over the two delivery vans at an agreed valuation of £4,000 each. Inventory (stock) is sold for £5,000 and trade receivables (trade debtors) have paid £8,000. Trade payables (trade creditors) are paid £4,000 and the costs of dissolution are £1,500.

Required

(a)   the bank account

(b)   the realisation account

(c)   the partners' capital accounts.

In this chapter you will learn how to:

- identify the main elements of published reports

- explain why companies publish their accounts

- demonstrate a knowledge of corporate report requirements of different user groups

- explain the limitations of published accounts

- prepare schedules of non-current assets

- explain the duties of directors and auditors with regard to the accounts.

Key terms

Non-current (fixed) assets: the term used for fixed assets which are expensive items bought not primarily to resell but to help generate profits.

Companies Act 1985, amended 1989 and 2006: these Acts govern limited companies and require that limited companies prepare and publish accounts annually. In 1989 EU directives (rules imposed by the European Union to harmonise accounting) were added.

Potential investors: are people who may wish to buy shares in a company. The element of risk and potential reward is important to this group and also whether they intend to invest for the short or long term.

You have already been introduced to this topic during the AS in Unit 2. Limited companies are required by law to produce financial statements (final accounts). Many companies have their financial statements (final accounts) on their website which means anyone can examine them. They can appear not to provide as much detail compared to those of a sole trader or partnership but this is because notes accompany the accounts which then give more detail, for example a schedule of **non-current (fixed) assets** which shows the non-current (fixed) assets bought and sold during the year and depreciation involved. The published accounts are not used for day-to-day decision-making within the actual business as they are a summary and the internal accounts will provide far more detail. You need to know the different user groups of the accounts and the limitations as well as possible uses for those groups. Directors have duties to perform in the process as do the auditors who are appointed by the shareholders to check the accounts produced. You do not need to be able to compile the published accounts but you need to have a good understanding of their content, purpose and who has responsibilities concerning them.

Case study

Roamaround Ltd is a newly established limited company. The two brothers who previously started their satellite navigation technology business as a partnership are aware that now they are a limited company they will have to publish their accounts in accordance with the Companies Act 1985 and 1989. They had just become familiar with trading, profit and loss accounts and are now faced with income statements instead and even the balance sheets look different.

■ Purpose of published accounts

Published accounts are regulated by the **Companies Act 1985, amended 1989**. Copies of published accounts must be sent to each shareholder and debenture holder. It is increasingly easy to access published accounts on company websites so they are firmly in the public domain. Annual returns must be completed and filed with the Registrar and kept at Companies House in Cardiff. In addition to the legal requirement, published accounts are used by shareholders and **potential investors** to allow them to make decisions, for example, whether to continue investing. A benefit of becoming a limited company is having limited liability. This means that unlike a sole trader or partnership, shareholders cannot lose their personal assets, only the amount of money they have invested in shares. The ability to raise far larger amounts of finance is also an advantage but there are legal obligations that come with the status:

- Financial statements (final accounts) must be audited (checked by a qualified accountant) to ensure a 'true and fair view'. This is not cheap and involves showing your financial statements (final accounts) to outsiders for scrutiny.

- Financial statements (final accounts) must be completed and filed with the Registrar of Companies.

Earnings per share

A useful ratio to assist potential investors is earnings per share (EPS) which is a published ratio.

To calculate the earnings per share we use the following:

$$\text{Earnings per share} = \frac{\text{profit after taxation and preference dividends in pence}}{\text{number of ordinary shares}}$$

The answer is expressed in pence. This represents the amount of return each share has made to its owner if all the profits available for distribution were to be paid as dividends. Of course any prudent business does not distribute all its profits, it will retain some for itself or transfer some to general reserves. The resulting figure, like most ratios, is meaningless if considered on its own although the higher the better for shareholders. The EPS result indicates the strength of an investment in the shares of one company when compared to another. Comparing it with previous years will determine if the amount per share earned is increasing or decreasing.

Table 1 *Summary*

	Dream plc	Clouds plc	Munchies plc
Net profit (after tax)	£2.2m	£3.4m	£5.6m
Number of shares	1,000	2,000	4,500

Users of published accounts

Table 2 *Possible users of published accounts*

User	Reason
Investors, potential investors	Whether to buy or sell shares, dividend payout
Pressure groups such as Greenpeace	Social accounting purposes, for example, how much pollution is the company creating, their carbon footprint, etc.
Competitors	Benchmarking performance
Banks and financial institutions	Lending risk can be assessed
Analysts	To make recommendations based on current and historic information
Trade payables (trade creditors)	Trading decisions such as how much credit to give or how much to lend

Limitations of published accounts

Whilst published accounts are widely available their actual value can be limited for the following reasons:

1 They are based on historical information and the figures may not reflect the current trading position, the economic situation such as low inflation or high interest rates. Published accounts take a long time to be produced and as soon as they are published are already several months out of date. Past performance is no guarantee of future performance.

2 Summarised figures hide the detail such as exactly how much is spent on advertising or on staff wages. This means it is hard to perform

Link

You have previously looked at the internal final accounts of limited companies in AS Unit 2 which will come in useful for this area. Be aware of the slightly different terminology used for published accounts.

Activities

1 Using the relevant chapters in this book, look at the financial statements (final accounts) for a partnership and the financial statements for a limited company and produce a report for the directors of Roamaround Ltd explaining the similarities and the differences between the two.

2 Calculate the earnings per share for each of the companies in Table 1 and from your results consider which company would potentially be the best investment opportunity on your evidence.

3 In pairs research a user group and examine the usefulness and limitations of published accounts to that group.

Key term

Analysts: their job is to closely examine trends, published accounts and the stock exchange where stocks and shares are bought and sold and make predictions.

specific benchmarking. For example, it would be very useful for a competitor to know exactly how much the company spends on their call centre in the Far East but this information is hidden under the umbrella of administration expenses so is impossible to know.

3 Window dressing occurs which is legal but means that a certain amount of massaging of figures may take place, presenting the company in the best possible light. For example, a revaluation of premises may have recently taken place to boost the non-current (fixed) assets on the balance sheet.

4 The human aspect such as labour turnover, absenteeism rates, is not included which can tell the user a lot about the morale and qualities such as qualifications and experience of the workforce that cannot be seen in the published accounts alone.

5 Not accessible/too complex for non-specialist users. Think back to when you first started studying accounting. Many of the terms are unfamiliar and also have several ways of being expressed for example revenue (sales), turnover and income.

Contents of published accounts

The contents are decided by the International Accounting Standards Board whose job it is to ensure that accounting standards help produce high quality, transparent and comparable accounts. For now we will concentrate on IAS 1 Presentation of financial statements (final accounts) which states that a set of financial statements (final accounts) contains:

- a balance sheet
- an income statement (trading and profit account)
- a **statement of changes in capital (equity)** for the period (this deals with any share issues, dividend paid etc.)
- a statement of cash flows (cash flow statement) for the period (covered by IAS 7)
- notes, comprising a summary of significant accounting policies and other explanatory information.

■ Illustration

Income statements

Roamaround Ltd Income Statement for the year ended 31 December 2008

	£ 000
Revenue	900
Cost of revenue (sales)	(400)
Gross profit	500
Distribution costs	(25)
Administration expenses	(30)
Profit from operations	445
Investment income	8
Finance cost	(13)
Profit before tax	440
Tax expense	(150)
Profit after tax	290

Fig. 5.1 *Income statement for Roamaround Ltd*

Link

The role of the International Accounting Standards Board will be examined in more depth in Chapter 7.

Key terms

Statement of changes in capital (equity): this section records the issue of shares.

Link

Chapter 6 deals with cash flow statements, IAS 7.

Most of the above terms should be familiar to you but here is a reminder:

- Revenue = sales, turnover less any sales returns/returns inwards.
- Cost of revenue (sales) = opening stock plus purchases and carriage inwards less purchase returns/returns outwards less closing stock.
- Gross profit = revenue less cost of sales.
- Distribution costs = costs involved in storing, packing and delivering goods to customers.
- Adminstration expenses = management and all other expenses such as advertising. Discounts allowed should be added to this category and discounts received subtracted.
- Profit from operations = gross profit less distribution costs and administration expenses.
- Investment income is interest received from any investment property (investments) the company may have.
- Finance cost is what is paid in interest on loans or overdrafts.
- Profit before tax = this is used to calculate the amount of corporation tax the company needs to pay.
- Tax expense = this cannot be known until the income statement is produced so also appears on the balance sheet as a current liability.
- Profit after tax = this is available to be distributed to shareholders or to be retained in the company.

Illustration

Statement of changes in capital (equity)

Roamaround Ltd Statement of changes in capital (equity) for the year ended 31 December 2008.

	£ 000
Balance 1 January 2008	5,469
Profit for the year	290
	5,759
Dividends paid	200
Balance 31 December 2008	5,559

Fig. 5.2 *Changes in equity*

Movements involving the shareholders are now in a separate statement as shown above. You can track the figures from the income statement (trading and profit and loss account) which is where the £290,000 profit for the year figure comes from on to the balance sheet where the closing balance of £5,559 is shown as retained earnings under the capital (equity) section. Also included under this heading would be any new issues of shares.

■ Illustration

Balance sheet

Roamaround Ltd Balance Sheet at 31 December 2008.

	£000	£000
ASSETS		
Non-current assets		
Property, plant and equipment	100,000	
Other intangible assets	20,000	
		120,000
Current assets		
Inventories	5,000	
Trade and other receivables	250	
Cash and cash equivalents	10	
		5,260
Total assets		125,260
Current liabilities		
Trade and other payables	(1,300)	
Short-term borrowings	(80)	
Current tax payable	(150)	
Short-term provisions	(171)	
	(1,701)	
Non-current liabilities		
Long-term borrowings	(30,000)	
Long-term provisions	(8,500)	
	(38,500)	
Total liabilities		(40,201)
Net assets		85,059
CAPITAL (EQUITY)		
Share capital		70,000
Share premium account		5,000
Revaluation account		4,500
Retained earnings		5,559
Total capital (equity)		85,059

Fig. 5.3 *Balance sheet*

There are more new terms in the balance sheet than income statement so they are listed below:

Table 3 *Current UK and international terms*

Current UK Term	International Standards Term
Fixed assets	Non-current assets
Land and buildings	Property
Goodwill, patents, copyrights	Other intangible assets
Stocks of raw materials and stocks of finished goods	Inventories
Trade receivables (debtors)	Trade and other receivables
Bank and cash	Cash and cash equivalents
Long-term liabilities, trade payables (creditors): amounts falling due within one year	Non-current liabilities
Trade creditors	Trade and other payables

Example of a company balance sheet

	2008 £m	2007 £m
Assets and liabilities		
Non-current assets		
Investments in subsidiaries	2,477.7	2,477.7
Other financial assets	0.5	1.9
Deferred tax asset	0.1	0.1
	2,478.3	2,479.7
Current assets		
Trade and other receivables	841.2	63.4
Current tax asset	10.3	6.3
Cash and short term deposits	0.4	66.7
	851.9	136.4
Total assets	3,330.2	2,616.1
Current liabilities		
Bank overdrafts	(30.0)	-
Unsecured bank loans	(205.0)	-
Trade and other payables	(12.8)	(10.0)
Other financial liabilities	(53.6)	-
	(301.4)	(10.0)
Non-current liabilities		
Corporate bonds	(539.7)	(531.2)
Other financial liabilities	(12.3)	(19.2)
Other liabilities	(0.5)	(1.8)
	(552.5)	(552.2)

(Continued)

Key terms

Inventory: stock for resale.

Trade and other receivables: this includes trade receivables (debtors) and prepayments, amounts owed to us or that we have paid ahead for, for example, rent and insurance.

Cash and cash equivalents: cash held on the premises or in the bank account.

Non-current liabilities: what the company owes and is due to be repaid after 12 months such as a loan.

Trade and other payables: what the company owes to trade creditors, and accruals being money owed, for example on wages.

Activity

4 Examine the company balance sheet shown for Next plc. What changes have occurred between 2007 and 2008? Explain possible causes for these changes. Research any of the entries which are unfamiliar to you.

Background knowledge

IAS 1 was revised in September 2007, so if you do examine some recent financial statements you may notice that the term 'balance sheet' has now been replaced with a 'statement of financial position'. You should continue to refer to it as a balance sheet in the examination.

Total liabilities	(853.9)	(562.2)
Net assets	2,476.3	2,053.9
CAPITAL (EQUITY)		
Share capital	20.1	22.7
Share premium account	0.7	0.7
Capital redemption reserve	9.8	7.2
ESOT reserve	(54.8)	(76.9)
Other reserves	985.2	985.2
Retained earnings	1,515.3	1,115.0
Total capital (equity)	2,476.3	2,053.9

Fig. 5.4 *Company balance sheet for next plc as at 26 January 2008*

■ Duties of directors and auditors

The **directors** are responsible for the whole process of completing the financial statements (final accounts). **Auditors** are independent of the company and act as an unbiased checking device that the declared financial information and company position is accurately reported. The role of the auditor is to form an opinion and declare whether a true and fair view is provided. They are entitled to any information they require to enable them to form an opinion. Auditors will never state that the financial statements (final accounts) are 100% accurate because they can only check the information the company provides them with. The true and fair opinion is based on the fact that the accounts contain estimates and are subject to a number of decisions. All auditors' reports state the same information and include:

- respective responsibilities of directors and auditors
- basis of audit opinion
- opinion.

If you look at different companies' auditors' reports you will see how similar they all are. Directors' reports on the other hand do vary as they are specifically reporting on the company involved. The report will look at the achievements of the past year, profits and dividends, the board of directors, employee involvement, equal opportunities, to name just a few. They also give notice of when the **annual general meeting (AGM)** will be held where shareholders get the chance to voice their opinions.

Schedule of non-current assets

A **schedule of non-current assets** is a summary of the non-current (fixed) assets and any new non-current (fixed) assets bought (additions), sold (disposals) and the depreciation attached to the disposals and the depreciation charge for this year. This allows us then to calculate the net book value which then appears on the balance sheet.

Illustration

Schedule of non-current assets

Schedule of non-current (fixed) assets for Triangle Nuts plc at
31 March 2008.

	Property £000	Fixtures, fittings and equipment £000
Cost at start	2,000	625
Revaluation	20	
Additions		130
Disposals		(100)
Cost at end	2,020	655
Depreciation at start	20	300
Disposals		(28)
Charge for year	15	55
Depreciation end of year	35	327
Net book value end of year	1,985	328

Fig. 5.5 *Example of a schedule of non-current (fixed) assets*

- Cost at start = the original cost of the non-current assets before depreciation is applied.
- Revaluation = how much the non-current (fixed) asset is increasing in value. The double entry is to debit (fixed) asset and credit revaluation reserve.
- Additions = any non-current (fixed) assets bought throughout the year, at cost.
- Disposals = any non-current (fixed) assets which have been sold during the year, at cost.
- Cost at end = the cost of the non-current assets (fixed) after any additions, disposals or revaluation taking place.
- Depreciation at start = the accumulated depreciation so far.
- Disposals = the depreciation attached to the non-current (fixed) assets which have been disposed of.
- Charge for the year = the depreciation for the year.
- Depreciation end of year = depreciation at start less disposals plus this year's depreciation charge.
- Net book value = cost at end less depreciation end of year. This is the amount which will appear on the balance sheet.

The important point to notice here is that all the movements in the top part are at cost. It does not matter how much the non-current (fixed) asset was sold for, the company accountant needs to subtract the cost at which the non-current (fixed) asset was bought. The accountant also needs to dispose of the depreciation which that non-current (fixed) asset had built up during the time the company had it. To do this the accountant must calculate each year's depreciation since the asset was purchased and then total them.

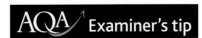

AQA Examiner's tip

A common exam question is to be asked the difference between the reports of the auditors and directors and the different criteria these two reports fulfil. You must ensure you are familiar with the reason for and role of the auditor in reporting on published accounts.

Stages in completing schedule of non-current (fixed) assets

1 Enter the cost of the non-current (fixed) assets at the start of the accounting period.

2 Has there been a revaluation? If so, make sure you include this. This will need adding to the cost at the start of an increase.

3 Disposals, these need to be removed at the price paid for them, the cost.

4 Additions, again it is the actual price paid, cost which needs to be shown and added in the same way as a revaluation.

5 You can now calculate the closing balance of the top half of the schedule which shows the closing cost of non-current (fixed) assets.

6 Depreciation, insert provision at the start of the year. This represents all the depreciation to date for the assets which the company still owns.

7 Disposal = cost – written down value (what the asset was worth after depreciation had been subtracted). You are removing any depreciation involving assets which have now been sold so this is subtracted.

8 Calculate the depreciation charge for this year and this will be added.

9 Calculate total depreciation charge by starting with the depreciation at the start of the year, less any disposals, add the charge for the year.

10 Finally the net book values are calculated which are the cost at the end of the year less the depreciation for the end of the year.

> **Activity**
>
> **5** Explain to the directors of Roamaround Ltd the purpose of a schedule of non-current (fixed) assets.

In this chapter you will have learnt:

- why companies publish their accounts, their limitations and how different user groups can use them

- the main elements in a set of published accounts and the new terminology according to IAS 1

- how to calculate and interpret earnings per share

- the duties of directors and auditors

- how to prepare a schedule of non-current assets.

AQA Examination-style questions

1   AQA January 2004
    (a)   Explain two reasons why public limited companies publish their accounts.
    (b)   Discuss two limitations for potential investors of using published accounts.

2   Distinguish between the roles of the auditors and the directors with regard to the published accounts.

3   The following data was taken from the published accounts of Dhiren plc for the year ended
    31 March 2008.

	£ 000
Property at cost	500
Machinery at cost	100
Office equipment at cost	20
Depreciation at 31 March 2007	
Machinery	15
Office equipment	6
Depreciation rates	
Machinery	25% reducing-balance
Office equipment	10% straight-line on cost

A full year's depreciation is charged in the year of purchase but none in the year of sale.
    i   During the year ended 31 March 2008 the following additions took place; machinery £10,000
         and office equipment £3,500. Property was revalued to £750,000.
    ii   Machinery bought in February 2004 for £2,000. The original cost was £16,000. Depreciated
                                                                                    by £9,000
Required
The schedule of non-current (fixed) assets for Dhiren plc for the year ended 31 March 2008.

4   The following data was taken from the accounting records of Blue Monkey plc for the year ended
    31 December 2008:

	Non-current assets at 1 January 2008	Depreciation at 1 January 2008	Non-current assets bought during 2008
Premises	700,000	-	-
Motor vehicles	120,000	35,000	22,000
Office equipment	80,000	12,000	38,000

Motor vehicles are depreciated at 15% reducing-balance method and office equipment at 5%
straight-line on cost. A full year's depreciation is provided in the year of purchase, but none in the
year of sale.

A motor vehicle bought in April 2004 was sold in June 2008 for £15,000. The original cost of the motor vehicle was £52,000. *Depreciated by £10,000*

During August 2008 office equipment, with an original cost of £12,500 and with a written down value of £6,200, was sold at a loss of £2,000.

On 2 February 2008 premises were revalued at £850,000.

Required

(a) The schedule of non-current (fixed) assets for Blue Monkey plc for the year ended 31 December 2008.

(b) Explain the purpose of a schedule of non-current (fixed) assets.

6 Statement of cash flow

In this chapter you will learn how to:

- prepare statements of cash flow (using the indirect method following the format given in IAS 7)

- explain the value of statements of cash flow to potential user groups

- comment on statements of cash flow.

Key terms

Statement of cash flow: this shows how cash has been generated (cash inflows) and how it has been spent (cash outflows), information not provided by the income statement or balance sheet.

IAS 7: the international standard we need to follow using the indirect method. Provides information about changes in cash and cash equivalents.

Indirect method: profit or loss is adjusted to determine operating cash flow.

A major cause of misunderstanding for non-specialists is how a company can have a profit of say, £2m but then also have a bank overdraft of £25,000. The reason for this is the difference between cash and profit due to the other payables (accruals) concept. The company may have yet to receive cash owed to them from trade receivables (trade debtors). They could have used cash to buy non-current (fixed) assets which only affect the profit through depreciation even though a large sum of cash may have left to pay for the assets. Financial statements (final accounts) show what **should** have happened rather than the physical movement of cash. **Statement of cash flow** serve the purpose of linking together the operating profit a company has made with its bank and cash equivalents position. Cash equivalents are short term, highly liquid investment property (investments) that are readily convertible to a known amount of cash. **IAS 7** enables companies to report their cash generation and absorption in a way which helps provide information to users who need to make decisions based on the financial statements. Do not confuse a Statement of cash flow with a cash flow forecast (cash budget). Statement of cash flows are looking backwards and cash flow forecasts, forwards. Essentially the statement of cash flow provides the link from the profit or loss on the income statement through to the cash and cash equivalents on the balance sheet. This process needs completing in three stages which we will now examine.

Case study

Move It plc is a company who manufacture electric vans for home shopping delivery. They have been very successful and now supply two of the major supermarkets. They recently opened a new factory to cope with the demand. The shareholders are confused by the fact that the company has made a profit of £1.2m but have a cash flow crisis and are asking the bank for further loans as they have exceeded their overdraft limit.

Calculation of operating profit

You will be familiar with this process as essentially you are working backwards (using the **indirect method**) to recreate the operating profit which you will have covered in Chapter 5. The first step is to find the company's operating profit for that year. This is not part of the statement of cash flow itself but is needed to form the basis of calculating the company's net cash position from its normal operating activities.

	£ 000
Profit after tax	203
Tax expense	20
Finance cost	8
Investment income	(3)
Operating profit	228

Fig. 6.1 *Calculation of operating profit*

Profit after tax is the amount of operating profit remaining after adjustments for tax, finance cost and investment income have taken place.

Tax expense is the amount we owe in corporation tax for this year. This cannot be calculated until we have completed the financial statements.

Finance cost is the amount paid for borrowing money, for example, interest and charges on loans or overdrafts.

The profit after tax is found by comparing the retained earnings on the balance sheet for the two years. If the retained profit has declined then this will be a negative figure. You are working backwards so need to add on the tax and the finance cost (interest paid) and then subtract the investment income (interest received). You will then end up with operating profit which needs to be taken on to the next process.

Activities

1 What reasons could explain the difference between Move It plc's profit and weak cash position?

2 Explain what will happen to operating cash flow if; inventory decreases, receivables decrease, payables/current liabilities increase and other current assets increase.

Key term

Net cash from operating activities: operating profit is adjusted for movements in receivables, inventory, etc., to obtain this figure.

Reconciliation of operating profit to net cash flow from operating activity

We now need to take our operating profit and make adjustments for non-cash expenses such as depreciation and profit or loss on disposal of non-current (fixed) assets. Working capital changes need to be included, apart from cash and bank. For example, have our trade receivables (trade debtors) increased or decreased? If they have decreased then we have more cash circulating so the difference needs adding and vice versa. Cash and cash equivalents do not appear here as that comes at the very end of the statement of cash flow.

Illustration

Here is an example of a reconciliation of operating profit to net cash flow from operating activity with explanations.

Table 1 *Reconciliation of operating profit to net cash flow from operating activity*

	Explanation	£m
Operating profit	From previous calculation	228
Add back Depreciation	Not a real cash expense	73
Gain on disposal of property, plant and equipment	Again, this is a book value where we compare the NBV with the price the asset is sold for	(2)
Adjust for working capital changes	Other payables (accruals) concept	
Inventory increase	Increasing inventory (stock) worsens cash flow as we are spending cash	(20)
Receivables increase	Not collecting debts worsens cash flow	(30)

Payables/current liabilities increase	Delaying payment to suppliers improves short-term cash flow but can lead to difficulties with suppliers	42
Other current assets decrease	Selling current asset Investment propety (investments) will improve cash flow	<u>83</u>
Cash from operations		374
Finance costs (interest paid)	This is for loans and overdrafts	(3)
Taxation paid	Look at **last** year's taxation in current liabilities on the balance sheet	(28)
Net cash from operating activities		343

A negative operating cash flow could be of concern. Operating activities should generate profit but when these profits are not backed by cash then there are questions to be asked as any cash borrowed must be repaid with interest. It could be the company are giving over generous credit terms in other words not receiving the cash they are owed until much later and as a result they are forced to borrow cash to make up the short-fall.

The statement of cash flow

The third stage of the process is the actual statement of cash flow. We need to take the operating cash flow we have previously worked out as our starting point.

■ Illustration

Statement of cash flow

Square Circles plc statement of cash flow for the year ended 31 March 2008.

	£ 000	£ 000
Net cash from operating activities		343
Cash flows from investing activities		
Purchase of non-current (fixed) assets	(25)	
Proceeds from sale of non-current (fixed) assets	3	
Interest received	3	
Dividends received	Nil	
Net cash used in investing activities		(19)
Cash flows from financing activities		
Proceeds of issue of equity share capital	12	
Repayment of share capital	(2)	
Proceeds from long-term borrowings	2	
Repayment of long-term borrowings	(1)	
Dividends paid	(2)	
Net cash used in financing activities		9
Net increase/(decrease) in cash and cash equivalents		333

Fig. 6.2 *Layout for statement of cash flow*

■ Link

You need to think back to AS Unit 2 where limited company accounts were first introduced but remember the changes in terminology you have seen in chapter 5 of this book. Internal and published financial statements are not the same!

■ Background knowledge

The notorious American company Enron had 16 occasions of positive earnings (profit) but only three times did they have positive cash flow. Analysts now claim that their demise was inevitable. You can see what happened in the DVD *Smartest Guys in the Room*. An internet search will reveal plenty of resources and information regarding this company and its situation.

AQA Examiner's tip

It is important that you remember and use the headings in the statement of cash flow. If you understand what they represent you will know what should be placed in that section.

■ Key terms

Operating activities: revenue-producing activities that are not investing or financing.

Investing activities: acquisition and disposal of non-current assets and investment property (investments) that are not cash equivalents.

Financing activities: changes in the equity capital and borrowings.

AQA Examiner's tip

If you are asked to prepare a statement of cash flow you will need to complete the first two stages of calculating the operating profit and reconciling this operating profit to the net cash flow before you can complete the statement of cash flow.

Net cash from operating activites has been calculated in the previous section.

Cash flows from investing activities show the non-current assets which have been bought and sold at cost. We are not concerned with the profit or loss on disposal of non-current (fixed) assets here. We want to know how much we actually paid or received for the non-current asset. The interest received and dividends received are last year's or interim and again what we have physically received.

Cash flows from financing activities are concerned with any capital (equity) share capital that has been issued and any shares that have been bought back (redeemed). It is likely that loans have been taken or repaid and this is represented by the proceeds and repayment of long-term borrowings. Debentures could form part of that section. The dividends paid are what has actually been paid, not what we intend to pay based on this year's income statement.

In the statement of cash flow you need to put in what has physically moved in cash terms. So, for example, the dividends paid are last year's plus any interim dividend that may have been paid this year. The proceeds from sale of equipment is the amount actually received for the sale so, even if a loss has been made we have still physically received cash. The final line should always be calculated using the changes on the balance sheet rather than the answer you calculate. You do not write both increase and decrease, if it is a positive figure it is an increase and a negative means a decrease. If you have compiled the cash flow correctly then the two figures will match! It is important to remember that it is the MOVEMENT of cash which has taken place.

Activity

3 Complete the table showing the net increase or decrease in cash.

AQA Examiner's tip

If you are unsure whether you need to add or subtract a figure think about what it is you are trying to calculate and the likely effect on profit or cash. For example an increase in inventories means that there is less cash so that is a decrease.

Illustration

	2007 £	2008 £	Amount £	Increase or decrease?
a Bank	5,050	7,825	2,775	Increase
b Bank Overdraft	15,900 0	0 7,400	23,300	Decrease
c Bank Overdraft	55,000 0	0 60,000		
d Bank Cash Overdraft	45,000 10,000 0	0 2,000 12,000		

Fig. 6.3 *Net increase/(decrease) in cash*

Illustration

Using the latest information from Move It plc a full typical examination question will now be completed.

	2008		2007	
ASSETS	£000	£000	£000	£000
Non-current (fixed) assets		7,233		5,602
Current assets				
Inventory (stock)	858		988	
Trade and other receivables	935		888	
Cash and cash equivalents	112		32	
	1,905		1,908	
Total assets		9,138		7,510
Current liabilities				
Trade and other payables	775		627	
Current tax payable	20		60	
	795		687	
Net current assets		1,110		1,221
Non-current liabilities				
Loan		213		413
Net assets		8,130		6,410
CAPITAL (EQUITY)				
Share capital		6,000		4,410
Share premium account		771		441
Revaluation reserve		1,074		1,074
Retained earnings		285		485
Total capital (equity)		8,130		6,410

Fig. 6.4 *Balance sheet for Move It plc at 31 December*

	£ 000
Cost	
At 1 January 2008	6,523
Additions	2,396
Disposals	(665)
At 31 December 2008	8,254
Depreciation	
At 1 January 2008	921
Charge for the year	165
Disposals	(65)
At 31 December 2008	1,021
Net book value	
At 1 January 2008	5,602
At 31 January 2008	7,233

Fig. 6.5 *Schedule of non-current (fixed) assets*

Additional information

The proceeds from the sale of non-current assets in 2008 were £666,000.

Calculating the operating profit

	£ 000
Retained loss for the year	(200)
Tax expense	20
Operating loss	(180)

Fig. 6.6 *Calculating operating profit*

To find the retained profit or loss for the year the retained earnings for 2007 needs to be subtracted from the 2008 figure, so, £285,000 – £485,000 = £200,000 loss.

The taxation is taken from 2008 as they represent the amounts we are still due to pay.

The operating loss of £180,000 will now be used in the second stage.

Reconciliation of operating profit to net cash flow from operating activities

	£ 000
Loss from operations	(180)
Adjustments for:	
Depreciation for the year	165
Gain on disposal of non-current assets	(66)
Decrease in inventories	130
Increase in trade receivables	(47)
Increase in trade payables	148
Cash from operations	150
Taxation paid	(60)
Net cash from operating activities	90

Fig. 6.7 *Reconciliation of operating profit to net cash flow*

The loss from operations of £180,000 was calculated in the previous section and this is the starting point.

Adjustments are then made which have the effect of either increasing or decreasing the cash in the business.

Depreciation for the year is found in the schedule of non-current assets and is £165,000, this needs adding back as it is a book entry and is not an actual movement of cash.

	£ 000
Cost	665
Depreciation to date	(65)
NBV	600
Proceeds	666
Profit on disposal	66

Fig. 6.8 *Calculation of profit on disposal*

The cost in the above calculation represents the disposal of non-current (fixed) assets at cost, what was paid for them initially. The depreciation for those non-current (fixed) assets then needs to be subtracted as otherwise the depreciation includes charges for non-current (fixed) assets which are no longer owned. This leaves the net book value which then needs to be compared with the proceeds of the sale to obtain the profit or loss on disposal. If the non-current (fixed) asset is sold for more than its net book value there is a profit as shown here and if it is sold for less there is a loss. This needs subtracting from the loss from operations because it is a book entry. The physical movement of cash takes place when the assets are bought and sold. The proceeds of £666,000 will appear in the actual statement of cash flow.

The decrease in inventory is added because it means an increase in cash in the business as the inventory amount has fallen so has been converted into cash.

The increase in trade receivables (trade payables) means that more cash is owed to Move It plc so this movement needs subtracting.

The increase in trade payables (trade creditors) means that Move It plc owes more cash so this is added because more cash is being retained in the company.

The taxation paid represents what was owed in 2007 accounts so is the amount which has now actually been paid. It is therefore subtracted since it will have decreased the cash.

The net cash from operating activities is the amount left after the adjustments. If it had been negative it would be called the net cash used in operating activities. This figure is now taken onto the statement of cash flow in the third and final section.

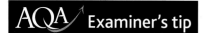

The statement of cash flow

Move It plc statement of cash flow for the year ended 31 December 2008.

	£ 000	£ 000
Net cash from operating activities		90
Cash flows from investing activities		
Purchase of non-current assets	(2,396)	
Proceeds from sale of non-current assets	666	
Net cash used in investing activities		(1,730)
Cash flows from financing activities		
Proceeds of issue of equity share capital	1,920	
Repayment of long-term borrowings	(200)	
Net cash used in financing activities		1,720
Net increase in cash and cash equivalents		80

Fig. 6.9 *Move It plc statement of cash flow*

The net cash from operating activities was calculated in the above section.

The purchase of non-current (fixed) assets is shown at cost and is the figure of additions from the schedule of non-current (fixed) assets.

The proceeds from revenue (sales) of non-current (fixed) assets is the cash received from the sale of non-current (fixed) assets and not the profit.

The net cash used in investing activities is the amount spent on non-current assets which is a negative figure as it represents a fall in cash plus any proceeds from the sale of non-current assets.

The next section examines financing activities, any shares bought or sold, loans or debentures taken or repaid. In the above case, Move It plc have increased their share capital by £1,920,000. This is found by subtracting 2007 share capital from 2008, 6,000,000 – 4,410,000 = £1,590,000 and then adding this to the increase in share premium. Remember, share premium is the additional amount which a share is sold for above its nominal or face value. In this case, 771,000 – 441,000 = £330,000. Add the two together, 1,590,000 + 330,000 = £1,920,000.

The net increase in cash and cash equivalents can be compared to the movement on the balance sheet which was £32,000 in 2007 and increased to £112,000 in 2008, a positive movement of £80,000.

Value to users of statement of cash flows

The movement to using IAS 7 to prepare statement of cash flows has simplified the process into three sections: operating, investing and financing. There is considerable flexibility as to which sections cash flows are allocated provided there is year-on-year consistency. Statement of cash flows can be a better indicator of liquidity than the other financial statements since they clearly show the **cash inflows** and **cash outflows**. There may well be some valid reasons why a company has a negative movement of cash. They may be expanding so purchasing larger amounts of non-current assets than they normally would. The statement of cash flow hopefully enables the user to examine the efficiency of how cash resources have been used that year. It can also be used to compare different companies which are of similar nature. A potential investor who is looking for a safe investment may value a healthy cash position as an indicator that the company can afford to pay dividends on a regular basis. Other investors may be looking for a longer commitment and be pleased to see considerable investment in non-current assets which will yield considerable profits and hopefully dividends in the future. Cash flow forecasts are more objective than the income statement as they examine the true cash flow movements rather than what should have happened. An income statement includes revenue which may never be paid so is more subjective than the actual cash position.

Uses of a statement of cash flow

1 Shows how a business has generated cash inflows.

2 Shows how a business has used cash resources during the year.

3 Inter-business comparisons can be made.

4 Highlights liquidity problems so that action can be taken such as securing an overdraft.

5 Shows movements in ordinary share capital and debentures.

6 Shows sources of internal funding and how reliant on external funding the company is.

7 Enables shareholders to see if the directors have used cash and resources sensibly.

In this chapter you will have learnt:

- how to prepare statement of cash flows using the indirect method following IAS 7

- how to explain the value of statement of cash flows to potential user groups

- how to comment on statement of cash flows by examining the three separate stages.

1 Explain how a company can make a loss but still have an increase in cash.

2 Discuss the extent to which cash is more significant for business survival than profit.

3 The following information has been extracted from the published accounts of Bump on Board plc for the year ended 31 December 2008.

	£ 000
Operating profit	32,874
Depreciation	3,890
Increase in inventories	20
Decrease in receivables	8
Increase in payables	4
Profit on disposal of property, plant and equipment	2

Required

Prepare the reconciliation of operating profit to net cash flow from operating activity for the year ended 31 December 2008.

4 Adapted from AQA Summer 2004.

The Financial Accountant of Adagio plc is in the process of drafting the financial statements for the year ended 30 April 2008. She has provided the following information for the preparation of a statement of cash flow.

	£ 000
Decrease in payables	1,787
Decrease in receivables	986
Decrease in inventories	48
Depreciation	3,490
Capital (equity) dividends paid	299
Loss on disposal of non-current assets	58
Operating loss for the year	2,127
Payments to acquire non-current assets	1,795
Receipts from sale of non-current assets	818
Taxation paid	278

Required

(a) Prepare a reconciliation of operating profit/loss to the net cash flow from operating activities.

(b) Prepare a statement of cash flow using IAS 7.

(c) Explain to what extent a statement of cash flow is essential in judging the financial performance of a company.

5   The summarised balance sheets of Fuschia Magic plc at 30 September 2008 are shown below.

	2007		2008	
ASSETS	£ 000	£ 000	£ 000	£ 000
Non-current (fixed) assets		350		400
Current assets				
Inventory (stock)	134		200	
Trade and other receivables (trade debtors)	150		180	
Cash and cash equivalents (bank and cash)	30		0	
	314		380	
Total assets		664		780
Current liabilities				
Trade and other payables (trade creditors)	(186)		(248)	
~~Short-term borrowings~~ *Bank overdraft*	0		(10)	
Current tax payable	(11)		(15)	
	(197)		(273)	
Net current assets		117		107
Net assets		467		507
CAPITAL (EQUITY)				
Share capital		350		375
~~Other~~ *Revaluation* reserves		45		50
Retained earnings		72		82
Total capital (equity)		467		507

There were no disposals of fixed assets and the depreciation for the year ended 2008 was £8,000.

Required

Prepare a statement of cash flow in accordance with IAS 7 for the year ended 30 September 2008.

6   The balance sheets for the last two years for Sheets of Paper plc are shown below:

	2007		2008	
ASSETS	£ 000	£ 000	£ 000	£ 000
Non-current (fixed) assets		405		310
Current assets				
Inventory (stock)	260		200	
Trade and other receivables (trade debtors)	82		62	
Cash and cash equivalents (bank and cash)	8		55	
	350		317	
Total assets		755		627

(Continued)

Current liabilities				
Trade and other payables (trade creditors)	165		167	
Short-term borrowings	39		0	
Current tax payable	63		52	
	267		219	
Net current assets		83		98
Non-current liabilities				
Loan		20		0
Net assets		468		408
CAPITAL (EQUITY)				
Share capital		230		200
Other reserves		72		72
Retained earnings		166		136
Total capital (equity)		468		408

Non-current (fixed) assets originally costing £20,000, net book value £5,000 were sold during the year for £9,000 cash.

An interim dividend of £25,000 was paid during the year.

Required

Prepare a statement of cash flow in accordance with IAS 7 for the year ended 30 April 2008.

7   Accounting standards

In this chapter you will learn how to:

- explain the purposes of accounting standards

- apply the main points of the standards you need to know

- apply each of the standards to particular situations described for a limited company.

Background knowledge

Some of the IASs were updated in September 2007 such as IAS 1 and IAS 10. The standards and explanations here are suitable for the current specification.

Key terms

Accounting standard: this allows financial statements to be compared over years and between companies.

International Accounting Standard: these are standards set by the International Accounting Standards Board.

Activity

1 A good way of learning something new is to teach it to someone else! Split the standards between the members of your group and each research a standard. Produce a PowerPoint presentation or an interesting handout which summarises the key points of the standards and present them to each other. You should then have a complete set of notes.

Accounting standards were introduced to bring comparability of financial statements between companies and to minimise creative accounting. Creative accounting involves companies showing their financial statements in the best possible light. This could be to attract potential investors. It is important that this practice is minimised with the use of accounting standards in order to allow sufficient comparability of financial statements between years and companies. There are two main areas of creative accounting:

1 manipulation of profit, showing profit as being on an upward trend and so good quality

2 manipulation of liabilities which involves the under-reporting of liabilities also known as off balance sheet finance.

As soon as one 'loophole' (way to be creative with financial statements) has been dealt with then companies will find another way to be creative, so, to deal with this, modern accounting standards are based on principles rather than rules. The International Accounting Standards Board (IASB) uses a framework which deals with:

- the objective of financial statements, to provide information about the financial position, performance and changes which are useful to users

- qualities that financial information should have for it to be useful

- definitions of the elements in financial statements (assets, liabilities, capital (equity), income and expenses) and their recognition and measurement.

Case study

Music Now Ltd

Music Now Ltd is a successful download music store which was previously a partnership between two friends, Wade and Trixy. Their accountant has advised them that their new status brings with it a considerable number of standards to comply with. Wade and Trixy are confused about IASs and why they should bother to adhere to them. Their accountant assures them that it is essential to follow the IASs and he will ensure that they are explained to them so that they can make the best decisions in the interest of the newly formed limited company.

Purpose and importance of international accounting standards

All listed companies (not just the ones on the London Stock Exchange) in the EU have to now prepare their financial statements following the **International Accounting Standards**. Each of the standards will be taken

IAS 1 Presentation of financial statements: sets out overall requirements for the presentation of financial statements.

IAS 7 Statements of cash flow: the international standard we need to follow using the indirect method. Provides information about changes in cash and cash equivalents.

IAS 2 Inventories: concerned with inventory (stock) as an asset and expense and how it is valued.

IAS 8 (accounting policies, changes in accounting estimates and errors) criteria for selecting and changing accounting policies.

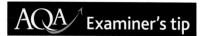

Examiner's tip

You do not need to know the standards word for word. You should have a good understanding of the key features and be able to match them to scenarios given using appropriate accounting terminology.

in turn and the key points explained. **IAS 1 Presentation of financial statements** and **IAS 7 Statements of cash flow** are covered in chapters 5 and 6 so will not be revisited here. Standards should enable financial statements to provide information that is useful in making economic decisions. The purpose of accounting standards is to address:

- Comparability – information provided for one period must be comparable with that provided for the previous period and between companies.
- Consistency – in order to achieve comparability, information must be given consistently from one period to another, and accounting policies must be fully disclosed.
- Understandability – users of financial statements are expected to have a reasonable knowledge of business and economic activities and accounting. This does not mean that a vital piece of information should be omitted just because it is complex.
- Relevant and reliable – there should not be major errors or any bias.

IAS 2 Inventories

Inventory (stock) is important as it is shown as an asset on the balance sheet and has a direct impact on the measurement of profit. Inventory can include:

- raw materials – materials to be used in production
- work in progress – goods in process of production
- finished goods – goods held for sale.

Prudence is an important concept with inventory as we must value inventory at the lower of cost (what we paid for it) or net realisable value (selling price – costs involved in repairing inventory into a saleable condition).

The cost of inventories comprises all:

- costs of purchases
- 'other costs' incurred in bringing the inventories to their present location and condition
- costs of conversion.

Take care with carriage – carriage inwards can be included in the cost of inventories but carriage outwards cannot. Inventories can be valued on the first in first out (FIFO) basis or using a weighted average method. Inventory (stock) valuation will be examined in chapter 8.

Case study

Music Now Ltd

Music Now Ltd sells a variety of inventory via their website to complement the music download area such as storage units. They need to ensure that all relevant costs such as carriage inwards are included in the cost.

IAS 8 Accounting policies, changes in accounting estimates and errors

IAS 8 addresses the criteria for selecting and changing accounting policies, together with the accounting treatments for changes in accounting policy and the correction of errors. The underlying issue here is that the information must be relevant and reliable.

Table 1 *Definitions needed for IAS 8*

Accounting policies	Prior period errors
Specific principles, bases, conventions, rules and practices applied by an entity in preparing and presenting financial statements.	The errors must be ones that were reasonably identifiable when the financial statements were authorised for issue.

Accounting policies must be applied consistently to similar events and transactions. Errors can arise from mistakes or misinterpretations. They must be corrected in the first set of financial statements (final accounts) issued after the discovery. Prior period errors must be restated as if the error has never happened. So, if you found an error with your stocktake you must go back and change the incorrect figure and follow this through to the latest set of financial statements (final accounts). It should look as if the new policy or correction has always been there.

Accounting principles are the broad concepts that are applied in the preparation of accounting statements outlined in IAS 1, for example prudence, other payables (accruals), consistency, etc.

Accounting bases are methods used by directors in the preparation of the accounting statements. They identify acceptable methods and are intended to reduce subjectivity, for example the use of historic cost or revaluation as the method used to value assets.

Examples of changes in accounting policies:

1 asset measurement changed from depreciated historic cost to revaluation
2 expenses reclassified from cost of revenue (sales) to administrative
3 legislation changes
4 a new accounting standard leads to change.

It is important to look at a company's choice of accounting policies when performing ratio analysis and interpreting financial statements (final accounts).

Case study

Music Now Ltd

Music Now Ltd discovered that when the stocktake took place an area of the stockroom had not been checked. This amounted to £5,500 of inventory. When this was discovered the financial statements were corrected under IAS 8 to reflect the true situation at the time of the stocktake.

IAS 10 Events after reporting period

IAS 10 explains the duties of companies and directors in looking for and adjusting for events after the reporting period. Companies have six months to file their accounts which can be a long time in the business world with some major changes happening such as a fire destroying one of your buildings.

Adjusting events – evidence of conditions that existed at the balance sheet date. **Adjust the accounts**.

> **Key term**
>
> **IAS 10 Events after reporting period:** these events may affect users' interpretation of the financial statements.

If the amount(s) involved are material, then the amounts shown in the financial statements should be changed.

Examples could include:

- A liability that existed at the year end, the value of which became clear after the balance sheet date.
- Where a customer has become insolvent after the balance sheet date and the large debt is included in the year end trade receivables.

Non-adjusting events – conditions that arise after the balance sheet date. **Disclose in the notes**.

If such events are material then they are disclosed by way of notes to the accounts. These notes would explain the nature of the event and if possible the likely financial consequences of the event.

Examples might include:

- A major restructuring of the business.
- Significant business commitments entered into after the balance sheet date.

For example, dividends declared after the balance sheet date are not recognised as a liability at the balance sheet date as they were not owing at that date, so no adjustment is made for them. Financial statements (final accounts) are usually prepared on the basis that the entity will continue as a going concern. If a decision to liquidate the entity or to cease trading is made after the balance sheet date, the going concern basis is no longer appropriate.

When events occur after the reporting period but before the date that the financial statements are authorised we need to know how best to handle them. We need to consider whether we have just been made aware of a condition that actually existed at the reporting period, in which case we do adjust, or if it arose after the reporting period there should be a disclosure in the notes. No changes can be made once the financial statements (final accounts) have been authorised.

> ### Activity
>
> **2** Decide whether to adjust or not following IAS 10 for the following scenarios which occurred after the balance sheet date:
>
> **a** a branch of the business was sold
>
> **b** inventory (stock) included on the balance sheet was sold below cost
>
> **c** major change in currency exchange rates.

Case study

Music Now Ltd

Two weeks after the financial year end Music Now Ltd bought out a smaller online business which serves the European market. This needs to be included as it is a significant restructuring for the business.

> ### Key term
>
> **IAS 16 Property, plant and equipment:** this concerns tangible assets held for more than one accounting period and used in the production or supply of goods and services, or for administration.

IAS 16 Property, plant and equipment

Property, plant and equipment are recorded initially at cost, which includes all expenditure to get the item ready for use. They are often a major item of expenditure for a company so need to be accounted for carefully to avoid producing misleading financial statements (final accounts). Expenditure on repairs and maintenance is classified as revenue expenditure and appears on the income statement. After it has been bought a company may choose to value the property, plant and equipment either at cost less accumulated depreciation, or at fair value due to a revaluation. Property, plant and equipment are depreciated over their expected useful life. The depreciation amount takes into account any expected residual amount. The method and rate are reviewed annually but should not be altered unless there is a good reason due to the consistency concept which allows comparison of financial statements (final accounts) with previous years. Freehold land is not depreciated. When an item of property, plant and equipment is disposed of, the profit or loss on disposal is included in the income statement.

Key information required:

- depreciation methods used (in our case, straight-line or reducing balance)
- useful economic lives or the depreciation rates used
- where material, the effect of a change of depreciation rate or method
- the cost or revalued amount of the assets
- the cumulative depreciation at the start and end
- a reconciliation of the movements of property, plant and equipment.

IAS 18 Revenue

IAS 18 is concerned with revenue (sales) from sale of goods, rendering of services and from the use by others of the company assets yielding interest, royalties and dividends. Usually revenue (sales) is recognised when it is likely that the economic benefits from the transaction will occur and can be measured. The realisation concept is behind this IAS which involves income only being recognised when it is certain.

Key term

IAS 18 Revenue: includes revenue from sale of goods, rendering of services and use by others of entity assets yielding interest, royalties and dividends.

Link

It is worth reminding yourself of the accounting concepts which you studied as part of AS Unit 2 as they play a considerable role in accounting standards.

Table 2 *Revenue and when it is recognised*

Revenue (sales)	Recognised
Sale of goods revenue	When significant risks and rewards have been transferred to the buyer; when the seller has no control over the goods
Rendering of services	Percentage of completion method or, the extent of expenses that are recoverable
Interest	Over time, on the effective yield on the product
Royalties	In accordance with the agreement
Dividends	When the shareholder has the right to receive payment

Timing is an important issue here, for example, sales with delayed delivery; subscriptions for products or fees for services delivered in parts over time. This is where 'window dressing' or creative accounting can occur in order to boost sales and hence profits. IAS 18 states that, if there is uncertainty about the possibility of return, revenue (sales) is recognised when the goods have been delivered and the period of time for rejection has expired.

Case study

Music Now Ltd

Music Now Ltd have decided to introduce a subscriptions service which means that new material can be downloaded before it is released on CD in the stores. Once the customer has used this service once then the period of time for rejection has expired and the profit can be recognised.

IAS 36 Impairment of assets

An asset must not be carried in the financial statements (final accounts) at more than the highest amount to be recovered through its use or sale. If that is the case the asset is impaired and the company must reduce the carrying amount of the asset to its recoverable amount and recognise an impairment loss, which is like an extra depreciation expense.

What could cause impairment?

- decline in an asset's market value
- adverse changes in the technological market, economic or legal environment
- increase in market interest rates
- obsolescence or damage of an asset
- plans to discontinue or restructure operations
- asset under-performance compared with expected return.

Goodwill and intangible assets with indefinite lives should be tested annually for impairment. The impairment losses should be charged to the income statement as an expense, unless the asset had previously been revalued upwards. If a revaluation has taken place then this must be removed. Sometimes a group of assets is considered rather than a single asset and this is known as a cash-generating unit.

IAS 37 Provisions, contingent liabilities and contingent assets

A provision is a liability of uncertain timing or amount.

A contingent liability is a possible obligation that arises from past events whose outcome is based on uncertain future events or an obligation that is not recognised because it is not probable, or cannot be measured reliably.

A contingent asset is a possible asset that arises from past events and whose existence will only be confirmed by uncertain future events not wholly within the control of the company. It would not be prudent to recognise income that may never be realised.

Table 3 *Requirements of contingent assets and liabilities*

Likeliness to occur	Liability of uncertain timing or amount	Asset of uncertain timing or amount
Virtually certain (therefore not contingent)	Make provision	Recognise (receivable)
Probable	Make provision	Disclose by note (contingent asset)
Possible	Disclose by note (contingent liability)	No disclosure
Remote	No disclosure	No disclosure

This IAS was introduced in response to creative accounting and originally it was felt that there was no need to have a standard concerning provisions. The measurement of a provision requires judgement about the amount, timing, and risks of the cash flows required to settle the obligation. Care is needed when making judgements under conditions of uncertainty.

IAS 38 Intangible assets

An intangible asset is one without physical substance. Intangible assets (goodwill) are either purchased or internally generated. Only purchased intangible assets (goodwill) can be recognised in the financial statements (final accounts), so internally generated intangible assets (goodwill) or brand names cannot be recognised. Intangible assets (goodwill) are shown in the financial statements in the same way that non-current (fixed) assets are. Intangible assets (goodwill) is the most common one but other examples include:

- Computer software
- Licences
- Trademarks
- Patents
- Films
- Copyrights
- Import quotas.

They should be recognised if it is likely that future economic benefits will flow to the company and the cost can be measured reliably. Purchased goodwill is covered by IFRS 3 Business combinations so should not be included in any answers concerned with IAS 38. The cost of generating an intangible asset internally is often difficult to distinguish from the cost of maintaining or improving the company's operations or goodwill. So, internally generated brands and customer lists are not intangible assets. Research expenditure is an expense and development expenditure needs to meet certain criteria to be an intangible asset. An intangible asset with a predicted useful life is amortised (written off in a similar way to depreciation) using the straight line method and those with an indefinite life are tested annually for impairment.

In this chapter you will have learnt:

- the purpose of accounting standards
- the key points of each of the IASs you need to know
- how to apply the standards to scenarios that a company may find itself in.

Key term

IAS 38 Intangible assets: non-monetary assets without physical substance.

Background knowledge

In 1998 Rank Hovis McDougall decided to put a range of internally developed brand names onto the balance sheet at a figure of £678 million. This became a new trend for companies which IAS 38 has now put a stop to!

AQA Examination-style questions

1   Explain the purpose and importance of accounting standards.

2   A company has spent £3 million establishing a brand name. The managing director wishes to include this on the next balance sheet and amortise it. Is this the appropriate treatment? Explain.

3   Hook Up have installed a new computer system at a cost of £3.5 million. The finance director believes that the installation and training costs of £1 million can also be included on the balance sheet. Is she correct?

4   According to IAS 2:

      'inventory should be valued at the lower of cost and net realisable value'.

      (a)   State three different types of expenditure that would be included in the valuation of inventory for a manufacturing company.

      (b)   Explain the effects that over-stating the cost of inventory would have on the financial statements of a company.

5   AQA Summer 2005

      The draft profit and loss account for Murray plc for the year ended 31 May 2005 showed a net profit of £1,355,675. The subsequent audit revealed a number of items where the accounting treatment did not comply with the international accounting standards and would affect the draft net profit.

      Items

- A batch of inventory (stock) had been included in the draft accounts at cost of £15,000. This had been damaged. It was estimated that the inventory (stock) could now be sold for £5,500, but the sale would incur costs of £500.

- Intangible assets (goodwill) on the balance sheet included £500,000 for internally generated brand names. There is no readily ascertainable market value for these brands.

- On 1 June 2004, the property was revalued. The revaluation increased the value by £400,000. Property is depreciated at 2% per annum using the straight line method. The depreciation charge for the year was based on the original cost.

- The accountant has not made a provision for doubtful debts this year. It is company policy to maintain a provision for doubtful debts of 3% of trade receivables (debtors). Trade receivables (debtors) have increased by £180,000 during the year, but no adjustment to the provision has been made in the income statement.

      Required

      State the relevant International Accounting Standard for each item and prepare a statement showing the effect of items on the draft profit.

8 Inventory (stock) valuation

In this chapter you will learn how to:

- calculate inventory (stock) values using FIFO and AVCO methods

- explain why different methods of inventory (stock) valuation produce different profit figures in the short term

- assess the benefits and drawbacks of using FIFO and AVCO

- reconcile inventory (stock) values with actual inventory (stock).

Background knowledge

Valuing inventory (stock) is important as it appears on both the income statement (trading, profit and loss account) and on the balance sheet. If the value placed on the closing inventory (stock) is too high then both the profit and the assets will be overstated and vice versa if the inventory (stock) is too low.

Key terms

JIT: just in time is an increasingly popular method of handling inventory (stock) where the minimum amount of inventory (stock) is held and replenished as required.

FIFO: the first in first out method involves the oldest costs being used first when inventory (stock) is issued.

Periodic method: this is when inventory (stock) is valued at the end of a financial period. It is the quickest method and should always be used when calculating the FIFO method even when perpetual is asked for as the same answer is found.

For many companies inventory (stock) can be a major part of the expenditure in the income statement and of the assets on the balance sheet. Some companies do seek to minimise the amount of inventory (stock) that they hold by using methods such as **just in time** (**JIT**), which means holding the bare minimum amount of inventory (stock) and thus avoiding issues such as storage costs, security costs, theft and items perishing or going out of date. The valuation of inventory (stock) is covered in IAS 2 Inventories and means that inventory (stock) should be valued at the lower of cost (what we paid and other associated costs such as carriage inwards) or net realisable value (expected selling price less any expenses to achieve saleable condition). As with the previous chapter on accounting standards it is worth refreshing your understanding of accounting concepts in particular prudence, consistency and the other payables (accruals) concept. It is important that these concepts are adhered to in order to produce the most accurate inventory (stock) valuation which is also acceptable by the Companies Act 1985 and IAS 2 Inventories.

Case study

Sharp Edges

Sharp Edges Ltd supplies chainsaws for tree surgeons. A new accountant has been appointed. The managing director would like the inventory (stock) of chainsaws to be valued at the price he intends to sell at. The accountant disagrees with this valuation but is concerned that the average cost method (AVCO) has been used which he considers to be more time consuming than first in first out (FIFO).

FIFO

First in first out, **FIFO** inventory (stock) valuation involves the assumption that the inventory (stock) bought first is used first. This is just in terms of the value of the inventory (stock) and does not mean that we must physically rotate our inventory (stock) (which a lot of companies do anyway). Any remaining inventory (stock) is valued much closer to the current cost using this method. FIFO produces the same result whether the **periodic** or **perpetual method** is used. The perpetual method involves keeping a running balance of inventory (stock) and its value which is more time consuming than the periodic method which is shown below. Always use the periodic method with FIFO as the result is the same and it takes less time.

Perpetual method: a running balance is kept using this method and a new value of inventory (stock) calculated each time inventory (stock) is received or issued.

AVCO: the weighted average cost method (also known as 'weighted average cost method') involves a new value of inventory (stock) being calculated each time a different cost is paid. This new cost is then used for issues until a new receipt of inventory (stock) is made.

Activities

1 Some companies such as Stoves Ltd who make ovens hold zero amounts of inventory (stock) as they have already sold the ovens that they are producing. What could be the advantages and disadvantages of this approach?

2 Explain to the managing director of Sharp Edges Ltd why the inventory (stock) cannot be valued at its selling price.

Illustration

First in first out method

The following information is available for Sharp Edges Ltd for the three months ended 30 June 2008.

On 1 April 2008 they had two chainsaws in inventory (stock) which had cost £20 each.

Date	Purchases	Revenue (sales)
3 April	3 @ £21	
6 April		2 @ £30
22 May	4 @ £22	
26 May		2 @ £30
9 June		1 @ £30
13 June	2 @ £23	

Fig. 8.1 *Inventory (stock) movements*

It is important to remember to include any opening inventory (stock) when performing inventory (stock) valuations. Unless you are required to calculate profit you must ignore the selling price of the inventory (stock) as this is irrelevant unless we can only sell the item for less than we bought it for.

	Units
Opening inventory (stock) if any	2
Add number of purchases/receipts	9
Less number of sales/issues	5
Closing inventory (stock)	6

Fig. 8.2 *FIFO method*

The table measures the inventory (stock) in units. Because we are using the FIFO method we have sold our 'oldest' inventory (stock) first so are now left with (2 @ £23 + 4 @ £22) = £134. Do not make the mistake of costing all 6 units at £23 as you only bought 2 at that cost.

FIFO is the most widely used inventory (stock) valuation method as it is the easiest to calculate and understand, it is acceptable for tax purposes and IAS 2 Inventories and the inventory (stock) remaining is valued at the most recent costs paid. This is useful for costing a job for a customer as it ensures we are using relevant and up-to-date costs to quote to the customer. This enables us to make profitable decisions in our planning. The issue costs of inventory (stock) are based on actual costs unlike AVCO which as you will see can produce costs that we never actually paid.

AVCO

The average cost method, **AVCO**, is just what is says: each time a new batch of inventory (stock) is purchased we need to calculate a new value for it based on average costs.

Illustration

Average cost method

	Received	Issued	Average cost per unit	Number in stock	Inventory (stock) balance
3 January	10 @ £18		£18	10	£180
12 January	15 @ £18.50		£18.30	25	£457.50
18 January		8 @ £18.30	£18.30	17	£311.10
22 January	8 @ £19		£18.524	25	£463.10
25 January		10 @			
30 January	9 @ £20				

Fig. 8.3 *AVCO method*

When we buy more inventory (stock) on 12 January we then need to recalculate. We do this by working out the total we have paid for inventory (stock) so far and then divide by the total number of units we now have.

$$\frac{(10 \times 18) + (15 \times £18.50)}{25} = £18.30$$

$10 \times 18 = 180$ is the amount of inventory (stock) we received on 3 January multiplied by the cost. This needs adding to the inventory (stock) on 12 January which is $15 \times 18.50 = £277.50$ giving a total of £457.50. Then divide 457.50 by 25 which is the amount of inventory (stock) in units, giving the answer of £18.30.

Activity

3 Complete the AVCO table for January in Fig. 8.3.

Advantages and disadvantages of AVCO

Table 1 *AVCO*

Advantages	Disadvantages
Recognises that all issues from inventory (stock) are of equal value	New calculation required with each purchase of inventory (stock)
Averages out changes in prices	Prices charged with issues will not agree with prices paid
Acceptable for tax purposes and IAS 2 Inventories	The profit which results is lower than the FIFO method

Effects on profit

In the long term the profits will be the same over the life of the company regardless of whether FIFO or AVCO are used as all inventory (stock) will be used up at all the prices paid for it. The difference comes in the short term where FIFO produces higher profits and AVCO lower. This may make you think, because of prudence, that it would be better to not overstate profits and use the AVCO method; both, though, are acceptable. What should not be done (in line with the concept of consistency) is frequent changes between the two as this then makes comparisons over years difficult. It is worth noting that the inventory (stock) valuation we use whilst affecting our profit does not affect our cash position. This is because we are still actually paying the same amount for the inventory (stock) regardless of how we then go on to value it.

AQA Examiner's tip

FIFO does not mean that we have to physically rotate the inventory (stock), it is the oldest cost of inventory (stock) we use first rather than the actual inventory (stock). A common error is that candidates confuse the physical movement of inventory (stock) with the inventory (stock) valuation for accounting purposes.

Activity

4 Advise the new accountant for Sharp Edges Ltd as to which method of inventory (stock) valuation he should use.

Illustration

Comparing FIFO and AVCO

The accountant for Sharp Edges Ltd has decided to compare the profit achieved for July using FIFO and AVCO to aid in his decision-making.

Date	Purchases	Revenue (sales)
6 July	6 @ £23	
10 July	2 @ £24	
15 July		4 @ £35
24 July	5 @ £26	

Fig. 8.4 *Inventory (stock) movements for July*

There were no units remaining at the start of July.

	Units
Opening inventory (stock) if any	0
Add number of purchases/receipts	13
Less number of sales/issues	4
Closing inventory (stock)	9

Fig. 8.5 *Method for FIFO*

Sharp Edges Ltd had 0 units at the start of the month, they purchased 13 and sold 4 so are left with 9 units, 5 @ £26, 2 @ £24 and 2 @ £23 so the closing inventory (stock) valuation using FIFO is £224.

	Received	Issued	Average cost per unit	Number in stock	Inventory (stock) balance
6 July	6 @ £23		£23	6	£138
10 July	2 @ £24		£23.25	8	£186
15 July		4 @ £23.25	£23.25	4	£93
24 July	5 @ £26		£24.78	9	£223

Fig. 8.6 *Method for AVCO*

The trading accounts can now be completed so that a comparison can be made.

	FIFO		AVCO	
	£	£	£	£
Revenue (sales)		140		140
Cost of revenue (sales)				
Purchases	316		316	
Less: closing inventory (stock)	(224)	92	(223)	93
Gross profit		48		47

Fig. 8.7 *Trading accounts to compare FIFO and AVCO*

Revenue (sales) is calculated by multiplying the number of units sold, 4 by the selling price of £35.

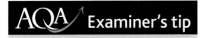

Examiner's tip

Do not use the selling price in your inventory (stock) valuation unless a trading account or profit is required. Remember that inventory (stock) must be valued at the lower of cost or net realisable value.

Activity

5 The new accountant for Sharp Edges Ltd has calculated the AVCO inventory (stock) balances and average costs per unit correctly as this method is unfamiliar to him.

Purchases are calculated by multiplying each order of inventory (stock) received by the cost so, $6 \times £23 = £138$, $2 \times £24 = £48$ and $5 \times £26 = £130$ totalled $= £316$.

Notice that the revenue (sales) and purchases are the same regardless of the inventory (stock) valuation method used.

The trading accounts show that gross profit is higher by £1 (£48 − £47), if the FIFO method is used. Total profits over the life of the business will be the same whichever method is chosen since all inventory (stock) will be sold.

Link

In AS Unit 2 you will have studied the key concepts needed for inventory (stock) valuation which are prudence, consistency and the other payables (accruals) concept. You will have also learnt mark up and margin which is useful for converting selling price back to cost price.

Stocktaking and the balance sheet date

In an ideal world all counting and valuing of inventory (stock) would take place on the last day of the accounting period. This is sometimes impossible so adjustments have to be made to discover the actual inventory (stock) held on the correct date. It could be that the stocktake is having to take place earlier than it should be and in this case adjustments are needed but the opposite way to the approach shown here. Always think about where the inventory (stock) should have been on the day of the stocktake and where it actually was. If it should have been included it needs adding and if it would not have been in the warehouse or stockroom it needs subtracting.

Illustration

Approach to adjusting inventory (stock)

Lozzie plc has a financial year end on 31 December 2008. The stocktake is not performed until 8 January 2009. The valuation on that date is £32,050. The following information is available:

1   Selling price is cost price + 25%.

   We must not calculate the inventory (stock) at selling price so will need to divide by 1.25 whenever we are given selling price to find the cost. If the mark up was 30% we would divide by 1.3 and so on.

2   Purchases since 31 December 2008 amounted to £4,500.

   Ask yourself where was that inventory (stock) on 31 December? Not in Lozzie plc's stockroom!

3   Returns inwards or sales returns since 31 December 2008 were £400 at selling price.

   Did we know on 31 December that we would be receiving this inventory (stock) back? No, so it needs subtracting. Remember to convert £400 to cost. So, $\frac{400}{1.25} = 320$.

4   Free samples of £57 had been included.

   Inventory (stock) should be valued at the lower of cost or net realisable value. If an item was free that makes its cost 0 so it should not be included in the inventory (stock) valuation.

5   Rain had damaged inventory (stock) which originally cost £600 and is now worth £80.

   Apply the same logic as you did in item 4. We need to subtract £520 to reflect the fall in value.

6   Goods with a selling price of £420 had been sent on a **sale or return** basis to one of Lozzie's customers on 20 December 2008.

   Sale or return is particularly useful for smaller businesses who

Key term

Sale or return: goods are supplied and do not need to be paid for until they are sold and can be returned to the supplier if they don't sell.

may not have enough finance to buy sufficient inventory (stock). It means that the seller displays the inventory (stock) and if they sell it they will pay the supplier and if they don't sell it after a certain time period they will return it to the supplier. Who does the inventory (stock) belong to on 31 December? Unless the customer has sold it it still belongs to Lozzie plc. Again, convert selling price to cost.

7   Invoices totalling £2,420 were sent out for goods sold during the first week in January 2009.

Where was that inventory (stock) on 31 December? In Lozzie plc's stockroom so it needs adding back after adjusting to the cost figure.

We can now enter the above information in the following statement.

Lozzie plc statement to show corrected inventory (stock) value at 31 December 2008

Valuation 8 January 2009			32,050
	£	£	£
	Increase	Decrease	
Purchases		4,500	
Sales returns		320	
Free samples		57	
Damaged inventory (stock)		520	
Sale or return	336		
Revenue (sales)	1,936		
Net increase/decrease	2,272	5,397	(3,125)
Inventory (stock) valuation at 31 December 2008			28,925

Fig. 8.8 *Adjusting inventory (stock)*

In this chapter you will have learnt:

- how to calculate inventory (stock) values using FIFO and AVCO
- the benefits and drawbacks of each method and how they affect the profit
- how to make adjustments for early or late stocktaking.

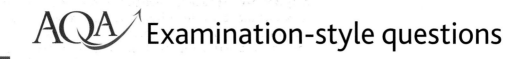

AQA Examination-style questions

1   Salema Begum owns and runs an office supplies business. She has always used the average cost (AVCO) method of inventory (stock) valuation. Her younger brother Rezah is studying accounting at college and is convinced that Salema could increase her profits by using the first in first out (FIFO) method.

   Required

   (a)   Assess the effect each of the two methods of inventory (stock) valuation would have on profits:

      i   in the short term

      ii   in the long term.

   (b)   Explain whether or not Salema should change the method of inventory (stock) valuation she has been using in order to alter:

      i   profits

      ii   cash flow.

2   Craig Taylor cannot decide whether to use FIFO or AVCO for his inventory (stock) valuation of his canisters in his scuba diving business and provides the following:

Date	Purchases	Revenue (sales)
1 September	10 @ £15	
2 September		4 @ £40
14 September	8 @ £17	
16 September	4 @ £18	
19 September		17 @ £40
24 September	9 @ £19	

   He had 2 canisters on 31 August which he had bought for £14.

   Required

   (a)   Calculate the closing inventory (stock) balance using both the FIFO and AVCO approaches.

   (b)   Prepare a trading account for each method, using your results from (a).

3   AQA Summer 2005

   Denise Watson sells one type of agricultural machine, a mini-baler. She provides the following information for April 2005.

   Denise had 2 mini-balers in stock at 1 April 2005. They cost £1,200 each.

Date	Purchases	Revenue (sales)
1 April	3 @ £1,200	
3 April		4 @ £2,900
7 April	4 @ £1,350	
17 April		4 @ £3,000
21 April	8 @ £1,400	
24 April		7 @ £3,000

Denise has calculated her gross profit to be £24,782, using the AVCO method. She sells her mini-balers in the order in which she purchases them. For this reason, she believes she should change her method of valuing inventory (stock) to FIFO.

Required

■ Calculate the value of inventory (stock) at 30 April 2005 using the FIFO method.

■ Prepare a trading account for the month of April 2005 using the FIFO method.

■ Discuss the advantages and disadvantages of both these methods of valuing inventory (stock). Advise Denise whether she should change her method of valuing inventory (stock).

4   AQA Summer 2002

The gardening section of a department store sells one type of ride-on lawnmower. The following information is available for the three months ended 31 May 2002.

On 1 March 2002 the store had one lawnmower in stock which had cost £1,600.

The following transactions took place between 1 March and 31 May 2002.

Date	Purchases	Revenue (sales)
16 March	2 @ £1,750	
4 April		2 @ £2,500
29 April	2 @ £1,850	
30 May		1 @ £2,500

Required

(a)   Calculate the value of inventory (stock) of ride-on lawnmowers as at 31 May 2002 using:

    i   the first in first out (FIFO) method

    ii   the weighted average cost (AVCO) method.

(b)   Explain **two** reasons why a business might favour the use of the first in first out (FIFO) method of valuing inventory (stock).

5   Always Friday plc has an accounting year ended 30 November 2008. At the end of November the store manager was ill and was unable to count the inventory (stock) until the close of business on 12 December 2008. At that date the inventory (stock) was valued at £105,980. The selling price of all goods is based on a 20% mark up on cost.

The following information relates to 1 December–12 December 2008.

    i   Included in the inventory (stock) valuation were goods at a cost of £1,200 which had been damaged and were now worth £500.

    ii   Sales invoices for goods sent in that period totalled £24,000.

    iii The company was sent a batch of free samples. They had been included at the price of £352.

    iv   Purchases of inventory (stock) were £12,500.

    v   Sales returned by customers were £5,200 at selling price.

    vi   The marketing department have currently borrowed inventory (stock) worth £600 for a trade fair.

Required

(a)   Calculate the value of closing inventory (stock) to be included in Always Friday plc's financial statements as at 30 November 2008.

6   AQA Summer 2003

Raymond Gilpan is a trader who uses a mark up on cost of 30% on all goods sold. He was unable to carry out a physical stocktake at his year end on 30 April 2003. He and his staff were able to complete the task one week later on 7 May 2003.

On 7 May 2003 Raymond's computer records showed closing stock valued at £7,600. However, the stocktake showed inventory (stock) valued at a cost of £7,420. This figure included a batch of damaged goods that cost £65. Raymond believes he can sell these goods for £80 after having repaired them at a cost of £20.

The following information relates to the period 1 May 2003 to 7 May 2003.

	£
Revenue (sales)	1,378
Purchases	NIL
Goods sent to Domkins on sale or return (selling price)	390
Goods returned to suppliers	110

Required

(a) Calculate the value of closing inventory (stock) to be included in Raymond's final accounts at 30 April 2003.

(b) Explain **two** reasons why the closing inventory (stock) as shown by a computer print-out may differ from that shown by a physical stocktake.

Further aspects of management accounting

Introduction to Unit 4

Unit 4 will develop your understanding and skills in relation to management accounting. For the first time you will look at organisations which manufacture products. Once you are familiar with the financial statements for manufacturing organisations, you will be able to move on to study a variety of costing concepts and techniques. For example, you will study marginal costing which enables appropriate decisions to be made when a variety of courses of action are available to a manufacturing organisation. This unit also introduces two techniques which are used by businesses when deciding how best to invest substantial amounts of finance in developing new products, replacing plant and equipment, etc. You will return to the subject of budgeting that was introduced in Unit 2 when you learned about cash budgets, but now look at other types of budget – for example, production budgets and labour budgets. Finally, you will investigate the wider context for business decision-making, and learn about some of the other, non-financial factors, including ethical factors, which might influence business decisions.

Chapter 9 – Manufacturing accounts

Will introduce manufacturing organisations. You will learn how to prepare end-of-year financial statements for manufacturers. You will study some sophisticated techniques which enable final accounts to be prepared which show not only gross and net profits, but the profit made from manufacturing as well.

Chapter 10 – Marginal costing

You will gain an understanding of how costs can be categorised and of important concepts including contribution, break-even and marginal cost. You will study techniques which enable businesses to make choices between alternative courses of action. For example, you will be able to decide which products a manufacturer should make when faced with a scarcity of certain resources, such as materials or skilled labour.

Chapter 11 – Absorption costing

Looks at absorption costing which is an alternative way of viewing manufacturing costs. You will learn how it is possible to make sure that all a business's costs are passed on to customers when pricing particular products or projects.

Chapter 12 – Activity based costing

A further method costing is covered in this chapter – activity based costing. This process produces more accurate cost information and enables management to have a greater understanding of why costs are incurred.

▦ Chapter 13 – Standard costing and variance analysis

Introduces the concept of standard costing. You will develop skills in using a technique, called variance analysis, which makes it possible for the management of a manufacturing organisation to identify unexpected changes in the cost of materials and labour. You will learn how to explain why such variations in cost might occur and how to calculate the effect of the changes on the budgeted profit of the organisation.

▦ Chapter 14 – Capital investment appraisal

You will study two techniques which help guide managers when choosing between alternative capital investment projects. You will learn how to calculate net cash flows for projects. You will then develop skills in assessing the impact of different projects, taking account of how quickly the money invested is paid back, and the real value of the cash flows taking account of the time value of money – the idea that money received some time in the future is not as valuable to an organisation as money received now. You will learn about the respective advantages and disadvantages of each technique and how to make recommendations as to which project should be chosen taking account of appropriate financial analysis.

▦ Chapter 15 – Budgeting

Returns to the subject of budgeting that was introduced in Unit 2 when you studied the reasons for budgeting and how to prepare a cash budget. In this chapter you will learn how to prepare a wide variety of budgets including those for receivables (debtors), payables (creditors), production, etc., and how they contribute to a business's master budget.

▦ Chapter 16 – Social accounting

You will look at business decisions from a wider point of view than just financial gain, taking account of how these decisions might affect various stakeholders including employees, and also the national economy, the environment, etc.

When you are assessed on this unit, you will be expected to demonstrate an understanding of the wide variety of techniques that have been covered, applying these to a variety of business problems. As always, well organised and presented answers will be expected. As you would expect in a unit which is much concerned with decision-making, you will also be expected to write explanations and reports in which you assess various courses of action. You will be assessed on how effectively you weigh up the benefits and potential disadvantages of the available options, and make recommendations drawing on the results of the analysis you have undertaken. As you know, at A2 level a generally higher standard is expected in all the skills on which you are assessed.

So far during your AS and A2 studies you have developed skills in preparing the accounts of several business structures: sole traders, partnerships and limited companies. These businesses have shared a common trait, namely they have all been retailers. However, not all businesses are retailers, whereby a completed good is purchased from a supplier and then sold on to a customer. Many businesses actually manufacture their own products which, when finished, are then sold on to customers. The final accounts for a manufacturing business differ to those of a retailer, as the costs associated with the manufacturing process have to be identified and recorded separately to the non-manufacturing costs. This chapter will introduce you to manufacturing companies and their accounts.

Topic 1 Introduction to the final accounts of a manufacturer

In this topic you will learn how to:

- prepare a manufacturing account showing the prime cost, work in progress and production cost of manufactured goods

- distinguish between direct and indirect costs

- prepare the financial statements (final accounts) and a balance sheet for a manufacturing organisation.

Key terms

Manufacturing account: an account prepared to calculate the production cost of manufactured goods.

Prime costs: the total of all direct costs incurred when producing the products.

Direct cost: is identified with the cost unit. Costs attributable to a particular product, e.g. direct materials and direct labour.

Case study

Matthias Manufacturing

Matthias Manufacturing Ltd produces wooden garden furniture. All products are manufactured within one factory and then sold to a variety of retailers from garden nurseries to well-known chain stores.

The manufacturing account

What is a manufacturing account?

A retailer buys and sells completed products, whereas a manufacturer has to produce the products to sell. A **manufacturing account** is therefore prepared to show all the costs associated with the making of these products within the factory.

A simple manufacturing account is split into two sections:

- the **prime cost** section, which calculates the total of the direct manufacturing cost of the products, and the **direct costs**, which include raw materials, direct labour and royalties

- the **manufacturing overheads** section which identifies all the other costs associated with the production of the products, for example factory rent, machine maintenance and machine depreciation.

When these sections are combined the **production cost of manufactured goods** can be found.

Illustration

How to prepare a simple manufacturing account from a trial balance

On 31 December 2008 an extract of the trial balance of Matthias Manufacturing Ltd was as follows.

Trial balance extract for Matthias Manufacturing Ltd at 31 December 2008

	£	£
Carriage inwards	2,200	
Carriage outwards	1,800	
Depreciation of manufacturing machinery	11,100	
Factory rent	20,100	
Manufacturing royalties	14,500	
Manufacturing wages	54,600	
Other factory overheads	32,000	
Purchases of raw materials	62,300	
Returns inwards	5,300	
Returns outwards		6,700
Revenue (sales)		234,000
Inventory (stock) of raw materials at 1 January 2008	17,400	
Inventory (stock) of raw materials at 31 December 2008	19,500	

Fig. 9.1 *Trial balance extract*

The manufacturing account for Matthias Manufacturing Ltd for the year ended 31 December 2008 was drawn up.

Manufacturing account for Matthias Manufacturing Ltd for year ended 31 December 2008

	£	£
Inventory (stock) of raw materials at 1 January 2008		17,400
Purchases of raw materials	62,300	
Carriage inwards	2,200	
Returns outwards	(6,700)	
Net purchases		57,800
		75,200
Stock of raw materials at 31 December 2008		(19,500)
Cost of raw materials consumed		55,700
Manufacturing wages		54,600
Manufacturing royalties		14,500
Prime cost		124,800

(Continued)

Key terms

Manufacturing overheads: the indirect costs incurred in the production of the products, for example depreciation of machinery, factory insurance and factory rent. These are often known as factory overheads.

Production cost of manufactured goods (also known as 'cost of production' or 'production cost of completed goods'): the total of all the costs of manufacturing the products.

Royalties: a sum of money paid to the inventor of a product for the right of use of his ideas.

Indirect costs: this cost is not identified with the cost unit. Costs which cannot be attributed to a particular product, e.g. indirect labour such as the wages of supervisory staff.

Activity

1 Identify three manufacturing businesses. For each business give three examples of an indirect cost.

AQA Examiner's tip

Ensure that the manufacturing account only includes information about the factory and actual manufacturing process and not other non-production costs such as warehouse, administration, finance or distribution costs.

Depreciation of manufacturing machinery		11,100
Factory rent		20,100
Other factory overheads		32,000
		188,000

Fig. 9.2 *Manufacturing account*

What is work in progress?

Manufacturing is a continuous process and so not all goods are complete at the end of financial period. The partly finished goods are referred to as inventory (stock) of **work in progress**.

The total production cost of manufactured goods in a manufacturing account is therefore made up of:

prime cost + factory overheads + opening work in progress – closing work in progress

Illustration

How to prepare a manufacturing account including inventory (stock) of work in progress

The inventory (stock) of work in progress for Matthias Manufacturing Ltd for the year ended 31 December 2008 were:

- inventory (stock) of work in progress at 1 January 2008: £12,500
- inventory (stock) of work in progress at 31 December 2008: £14,200.

Manufacturing account continued for Matthias Manufacturing Ltd for year ended 31 December 2008

	£
b/fwd	188,000
Inventory (stock) of work in progress at 1 January 2008	12,500
Inventory (stock) of work in progress at 31 December 2008	(14,200)
Production cost of manufactured goods	186,300

Fig. 9.3 *Manufacturing account continued*

Income statement

Preparing a manufacturer's income statement (trading account)

At the end of the production process the total production cost of manufactured goods is transferred to the income statement (trading account). This figure replaces the purchases of goods for resale within the calculation of cost of sales (cost of goods sold).

The completed goods are referred to as **finished goods**. These are placed in the income statement (trading account) within the calculation of cost of sales (cost of goods sold).

Illustration

How to prepare an income statement for a manufacturing business

The inventory (stock) of finished goods for Matthias Manufacturing Ltd for the year ended 31 December 2008 were:

- inventory (stock) of finished goods at 1 January 2008: £25,100
- inventory (stock) of finished goods at 31 December 2008: £29,400.

Income statement (trading account) for Matthias Manufacturing Ltd for the year ended 31 December 2008

	£	£
Revenue (sales)		234,000
Returns inwards		(5,300)
Net revenue (sales)		228,700
Opening inventory (stock) of finished goods	25,100	
Production cost of manufactured goods	186,300	
	211,400	
Closing inventory (stock) of finished goods	(29,400)	
Cost of sales (cost of goods sold)		(182,000)
Gross profit		46,700

Fig. 9.4 *Income statement (trading account)*

Balance sheet

How is inventory (stock) recorded in the balance sheet of a manufacturer compared to that of a retailer?

There are *three* types of inventory (stock) within a manufacturing business:

- inventory (stock) of raw materials
- inventory (stock) of work in progress
- inventory (stock) of finished goods.

The balance sheet for a manufacturing business therefore has to show all three types of inventory (stock) held at the year end within the current assets, whereas a retailer has only *one* type of inventory (stock), namely finished goods.

Balance sheet extract for Matthias Manufacturing Ltd at 31 December 2008

	£
Current assets:	
Inventory (stock) of raw materials	19,500
Inventory (stock) of work in progress	14,200
Inventory (stock) of finished goods	29,400
	63,100

Fig. 9.5 *Balance sheet extract*

All of the inventory (stock) in the current assets is valued at the lower of cost and net realisable value. This continues the application of the prudence and realisation concepts. This will further be illustrated in the next topic on unrealised profit.

In this topic you will have learnt:

■ how to prepare a manufacturing account to show the important subtotals, including prime cost and total overheads

■ how to distinguish between direct costs and indirect costs

■ how to prepare a manufacturing account to include work in progress

■ how to prepare a full set of financial statements (final accounts) and a balance sheet for a manufacturing organisation.

 **Examination-style questions**

1 Identify which of the following costs are either direct or indirect manufacturing costs.

Cost	Direct	Indirect
Cost of raw materials		
Factory supervisor salary		
Lease of factory		
Machine depreciation		
Royalties		

2 The following information is available for Blaker Ltd, a manufacturer of toys, for the year ended 31 March 2008.

	£
Direct wages	33,600
Factory overheads	16,500
Purchases of raw materials	21,000
Royalties	5,100
Other direct costs	1,800
Inventory (stock) of raw materials at 1 April 2007	6,200
Inventory (stock) of raw materials at 31 March 2008	7,400

Prepare an extract from the manufacturing account to show the prime cost for the year ended 31 March 2008.

3   AQA 2003 Jun ACC3 Q7

Norris plc is a manufacturing business. The following figures have been extracted from the company's ledgers as at 31 May 2003.

	£
Inventory (stock) as at 1 June 2002:	
Raw materials	21,450
Work in progress	14,780
Finished goods	58,620
Revenue (sales)	657,000
Purchases of raw materials	234,090
Direct labour costs	260,000
Indirect labour costs	82,800
Factory overheads (excluding labour costs)	138,000
Manufacturing royalties	6,560
Returns inwards	1,000
Returns outwards	980
Carriage inwards	750
Carriage outwards	1,340

Additional information:

■   At 31 May 2003, inventory (stock) were valued as follows.

	£
Raw material	22,170
Work in progress	13,750
Finished goods	60,650

■   At 31 May 2003 factory wages accrued and unpaid amounted to £8,000. One quarter of this was for indirect labour and the remainder was for direct labour.
■   Provision for depreciation of factory machinery for the year was £25,000.

Required

(a)   Selecting from the information given, prepare an extract from the manufacturing account for the year ended 31 May 2003 to show prime cost.

(b)   Explain what is meant by 'work in progress'.

4   Niklas plc manufacturers rugby boots. The following information is available for Niklas plc for the year ended 31 January 2007.

	£000
Carriage inwards	15
Carriage outwards	21
Factory wages	460
Heating and lighting	68
Machinery at cost	340
Office equipment at cost	90
Office salaries	245
Power	110
Purchases of raw materials	567
Rent and rates	84
Royalties	16
Revenue (sales)	1,246
Inventory (stock) at 1 February 2007:	
Raw materials	42
Work in progress	18
Finished goods	132

Additional information:

- The inventory (stock) at 31 January 2008 were as follows.

	£000
Raw material	65
Work in progress	22
Finished goods	146

- 60% of the factory wages are direct and the rest are indirect
- 75% of both the heating and lighting and rent and rates are to be allocated to the factory and the rest to the office
- 80% of the power costs are to be allocated to the factory
- depreciation is to be charged on the machinery at 20% per annum using the straight line method
- depreciation is to be charged on the office equipment at 10% per annum using the straight line method.

(a)   Prepare a manufacturing account for the year ended 31 January 2008.

(b)   Prepare an income statement for the year ended 31 January 2008.

(c)   Prepare an extract from the balance sheet as at 31 January 2008 to show the inventories (stocks) held at the year end.

Topic 2 Manufacturing profit

In this topic you will learn how to:

- explain why some manufacturers include a manufacturing profit

- prepare the financial statements (final accounts) of a manufacturer to include manufacturing profit

- explain why it is necessary to make a provision for unrealised profit

- calculate the provision for unrealised profit

- prepare the financial statements (final accounts) of a manufacturer to include entries for both the manufacturing profit and the change in the provision for unrealised profit

- prepare a balance sheet recording inventory (stock) adjusted for the provision for unrealised profit.

Key terms

Transfer price: production cost of completed goods plus a percentage mark up.

Factory profit, or manufacturing profit: the difference between the transfer price and the production cost of completed goods, or the amount of mark-up.

Link

For more information on mark up, see *AQA AS Accounting*, Chapter 9.

Case study

Danil Doors Manufacturing Ltd

Case study: Danil Doors Manufacturing Ltd produces wooden doors. All doors are sold to the national market.

The recording of manufacturing profit

What is manufacturing profit?

Some manufacturing businesses transfer their products from the factory to the income statement (trading account) at total production cost plus a notional mark-up percentage. This is referred to as the **transfer price**. The difference between the production cost of completed goods and the transfer price is called **factory profit, or manufacturing profit**.

What are the benefits of using a transfer price?

- This process does not increase the overall profits of the business and merely identifies the profit made by particular cost centres.

- In this way the profit from the manufacturing is separated from the trading profit made elsewhere within the business. The part that the factory contributes to the overall profitability of the business is recognised.

- This allows the unit cost of goods manufactured to be compared with the cost of buying in completed goods from an outside source and enables a manager to evaluate a 'make or buy' decision.

What are the drawbacks of using a transfer price?

- The profit loaded transfer price should be realistic so direct comparisons with the cost of buying in goods can be made. However there is a risk of an unrealistic view of the factory profitability being given unless other production prices are researched and used to set the transfer price.

- This technique does not improve overall the profitability of the business, rather it just splits the total profit between different cost centres.

- If a set percentage is used to calculate the transfer price this may fail to motivate factory managers and other workers, especially if their bonuses are dependent on the amount of factory profit.

Recording manufacturing profit

A manufacturing profit is recorded at the end of the manufacturing account. The transfer price then replaces purchases of goods for resale within the income statement (trading account).

Illustration

How to prepare a manufacturing account with a manufacturing profit and a transfer price

Danil Doors Manufacturing Ltd transfer doors from the factory to the income statement (trading account) at cost plus 20%.

On 31 March 2009 the company's trial balance was as follows.

Information for Danil Doors Manufacturing Ltd for year ended 31 March 2009

	£
Factory overheads	257,600
Inventory (stock) of finished goods at 1 April 2008 (at cost plus 20%)	108,000
Inventory (stock) of finished goods at 31 March 2009 (at cost plus 20%)	126,000
Inventory (stock) of raw materials at 1 April 2008	63,400
Inventory (stock) of raw materials at 31 March 2009	71,200
Inventory (stock) of work in progress at 1 April 2008	16,400
Inventory (stock) of work in progress at 31 March 2009	18,100
Provision for unrealised profit at 1 April 2008	1,800
Purchases of raw materials	220,900
Revenue (sales)	1,210,000
Wages	390,000

Fig. 9.6 *Trial balance*

Additional information:

- Wages owed amounted to £10,000.
- The wages are apportioned $\frac{3}{4}$ to direct labour and the rest is indirect.

The manufacturing account for Danil Doors Manufacturing Ltd for the year ended 31 March 2009 was drawn up.

Explanatory note

In previous illustrations the manufacturing account finished at production cost of manufactured goods. In this illustration goods are transferred to the income statement (trading account) at cost plus 20%. Two extra lines are therefore added at the end of the manufacturing account, namely

- factory profit: the amount of mark-up, in this example 20% of the production cost
- transfer price: the production cost of manufactured goods plus the factory profit.

AQA Examiner's tip

Ensure that the labels 'factory profit' and 'transfer price' are clearly shown at the end of the manufacturing account, as often the examiner allocates marks for the use of these labels.

Manufacturing account for Danil Doors Manufacturing Ltd for the year ended 31 March 2009

	£
Inventory (stock) of raw materials at 1 April 2008	63,400
Purchases of raw materials	220,900
Inventory (stock) of raw materials at 31 March 2009	(71,200)
Raw materials consumed	213,100
Direct wages	300,000
Prime cost	513,100
Indirect wages	100,000
Factory overheads	257,600
	870,700
Inventory (stock) of work in progress at 1 April 2008	16,400
Inventory (stock) of work in progress at 31 March 2009	(18,100)
Production cost of manufactured goods	869,000
Factory profit at 20%	173,800
Transfer price	1,042,800

Fig. 9.7 *Manufacturing account*

The provision for unrealised profit

Why is it necessary to create a provision for unrealised profit?

Standard accounting practice requires that inventory (stock) is valued at the lower of cost and net realisable value. In the balance sheet inventories (stocks) of finished goods should be shown at the cost of production and therefore if a transfer price is used these inventories (stocks) will include an element of **unrealised profit on finished goods**. Unrealised profits should not be recognised within the balance sheet and final accounts as it contravenes both the realisation and prudence concepts.

A provision for unrealised profit is therefore used to:

- remove the unrealised profit in the income statement (trading, profit and loss account) otherwise profits are overstated by the amount of unrealised profit
- remove the unrealised profit from the inventory (stock) of finished goods within the current assets on the balance sheet so that inventory (stock) is not overvalued and is valued at cost and not cost plus a percentage mark-up.

How is a provision for unrealised profit calculated?

When inventory (stock) of finished goods are valued at cost plus a percentage mark-up, the method for calculating the unrealised profit is

$$\frac{\text{inventory (stock) at cost plus profit percentage}}{100 + \text{profit percentage}} \times \text{percentage}$$

Illustration

How to calculate unrealised profit

At 31 March 2009 the inventory (stock) of finished goods was valued at £126,000, being cost plus the mark-up of 20%.

The amount of unrealised profit is therefore

$$\frac{£126,000}{(100 + 20)} \times 20 = £21,000$$

This approach can also be used to calculate the original cost of the inventory (stock).

In the previous illustration the original cost of the inventory (stock) is

$$\frac{£126,000}{120} \times 100 = £105,000$$

These answers can be checked.

cost of inventory (stock) + unrealised profit = inventory (stock) of finished goods at cost plus mark-up percentage

£105,000 + £21,000 = £126,000

Key term

Unrealised profit on finished goods: profit which is not recognised until the inventory (stock) is sold and a contract of sale has been negotiated.

Link

For further information on the prudence and realisation concepts and the valuation of inventory (stock), see *AQA AS Accounting*, Chapter 6.

Background knowledge

The realisation concept states that revenue should only be recorded in the business books of account when the goods have been sold for credit or cash and the prudence concept states that losses should be provided for as soon as they are anticipated, but profits are not recorded until they are realised as it is preferred for profits to be understated than overstated.

Explanatory note

This approach should be learnt. The percentage added to the denominator is always the same as the percentage by which the calculation is multiplied, namely the mark-up percentage. In this illustration it is 20%.

Explanatory note

The difference between the two approaches is only the amount by which the calculation is multiplied, either 20 for the unrealised profit or 100 for the original cost of the inventory (stock).

Activity

2 Calculate the amount of unrealised profit which is included in the following inventory (stock) values.

Table 1 *Inventory (stock) values*

Inventory (stock) values	Mark-up percentage
£	%
42,000	20
195,000	30

How is the provision for unrealised profit recorded in the balance sheet?

The inventory (stock) of finished goods is recorded at the cost price without the unrealised profit.

Illustration

How to record provision for unrealised profit in the balance sheet

An extract to show the inventory (stock) of finished goods in the balance sheet would be as follows.

Balance sheet extract for Danil Doors Manufacturing Ltd at 31 March 2009

	£	£
Current assets:		
Inventory (stock) of raw materials		71,200
Inventory (stock) of work in progress		18,100
Inventory (stock) of finished goods	126,000	
Less provision for unrealised profit	(21,000)	
		105,000
		194,300

Fig. 9.8 *Balance sheet extract*

Explanatory note

Whenever completing the current assets the original cost of inventory (stock) of finished goods should always be clearly identified. In this illustration it is £105,000. This complies with SSAP9 and the prudence and realisation concepts.

How is the provision for unrealised profit recorded in the income statement?

The provision for unrealised profit is recorded in the income statement (profit and loss account) as follows.

Table 2 *Provision for unrealised profit*

First year	Full amount subtracted from factory profit
Subsequent years	Increase in provision subtracted from factory profit
	Decrease in provision added to factory profit

Illustration

How to record provision for unrealised profit in the income statement

At 31 March 2008 the closing inventory (stock) for Danil Doors Manufacturing Ltd had been valued at £108,000, which included unrealised profit of £18,000.

The change in provision is recorded as follows.

	£
Last year's provision for unrealised profit	18,000
This year's provision for unrealised profit	21,000
Increase in provision	3,000

Fig. 9.9 *Change in provision*

This would be recorded in the income statement (trading account) as follows.

Income statement (trading account) for Danil Doors Manufacturing Ltd for the year ended 31 March 2009

	£	£
Revenue (sales)		1,210,000
Opening inventory (stock) of finished goods	90,000	
Transfer price	1,042,800	
Closing inventory (stock) of finished goods	(105,000)	
Cost of sales (cost of goods sold)		(1,027,800)
Gross profit		182,200
Factory profit	173,800	
Less increase in provision for unrealised profit	(3,000)	
		170,800

Fig. 9.10 *Income statement*

Explanatory notes

- Factory profit: This must clearly be identified within the final accounts as otherwise the profit is understated due to the inclusion of the transfer price instead of the production cost of manufactured goods.

- Increase in provision in unrealised profit: The increase in the provision in unrealised profit must also be clearly identified otherwise the factory profit is overstated. If there is a decrease in the provision then it should be added otherwise the factory profit is understated.

In this topic you have learnt:

- why some manufacturers calculate a manufacturing profit
- to prepare a manufacturing account to include manufacturing profit
- why it is necessary to make a provision for unrealised profit
- how to calculate a provision for unrealised profit
- how to record a change in the provision for unrealised profit in the financial statement (final accounts) of a manufacturer
- how to record inventory (stock) adjusted for unrealised profit in the balance sheet.

AQA Examiner's tip

A common error in the examination is either to forget to bring forward the factory profit or to show the change in provision in isolation. These two adjustments should be recorded together.

1   State the concepts identified with the provision for unrealised profit.
    Concept 1...............................
    Concept 2...............................

2   Nikoloz Ltd manufactures a single product. His goods are transferred from the factory at cost plus 25%.
    The following information is available at 31 October 2008.

	£
Inventory (stock) of finished goods at cost plus 25%	42,000
Inventory (stock) of raw materials	16,100
Inventory (stock) of work in progress	23,800

    Prepare a balance sheet extract to show the inventory (stock) held by Nikoloz Ltd at 31 October 2008.

3   Complete the following table.

Inventory (stock) at cost	Mark-up	Inventory (stock) at transfer price
£	%	£
12,000	20	?
26,000	40	?
?	25	50,000
?	10	33,000

4   AQA 2003 Jan ACC3 Q4
    Tecyl Products is a manufacturing business. It transfers all goods manufactured to the income statement (trading account) at production cost plus 20%.

The following figures relate to inventory (stock) held by the business.

	As at 1 December 2002	As at 30 November 2003
	£	£
Inventories (stocks) of:		
Raw materials	27,000	28,000
Work in progress	9,000	8,500
Finished goods	22,200	23,400
Provision for unrealised profit	3,700	3,900

Required

(a)   Calculate the amount of provision for unrealised profit to be entered in the income statement (trading account) for the year ended 30 November 2003.

The profit and loss entry is £.........................

What effect will the change have on the gross profit?

(b)   Show in detail how the information relating to all inventory (stock) should be shown on the balance sheet as at 30 November 2003.

Balance sheet extract for Tecyl Products as at 30 November 2003	
	£
Current assets: inventory (stock):	

(c)   Explain why it is necessary for Tecyl Products to provide for unrealised profit.

5   AQA 2005 Jun ACC3 Q5

Explain two reasons why a manufacturing business transfers goods to the income statement (trading account) at cost plus a mark-up.

6   AQA 2008 Jan ACC3 Q3

Donna Reayt owns and runs a manufacturing business. Goods are transferred from the manufacturing account to the income statement (trading account) at cost plus 30%. Donna provides the following information for the year ended 31 December 2007.

	£
Inventory (stock) of raw materials at:	
1 January 2007 (at cost)	14,700
31 December 2007 (at cost)	15,900
Inventory (stock) of work in progress (see the sixth bullet point below)	
Inventory (stock) of finished goods at:	
1 January 2007 (at cost plus 30%)	22,100
31 December 2007 (at cost plus 30 %)	24,700
Revenue (sales)	1,200,000
Purchases of raw materials	317,600
Carriage inwards	1,450
Carriage outwards	2,375
Wages	361,665
Manufacturing royalties	22,000
Factory rent, rates and insurances	16,200
General factory overheads	33,045
Manufacturing machinery at cost	300,000
Provision for depreciation of manufacturing machinery at 1 January 2007	180,000
Provision for unrealised profit at 1 January 2007	5,100

Additional information at 31 December 2007:

- Manufacturing royalties paid in advance amounted to £500.
- Wages are apportioned $\frac{2}{3}$ to direct labour and $\frac{1}{3}$ to indirect labour.
- Insurances paid in advance amounted to £900.
- Rates owed amounted to £850.
- Depreciation is to be charged at 10% per annum on a straight-line basis.
- Work in progress has decreased by £900 over the year.

Required

(a)   Prepare a manufacturing account for the year ended 31 December 2007.

Donna has prepared an income statement (trading account) using the information given. She has calculated her gross profit on trading to be £214,600.

Required

(b)   Calculate the amount to be entered in the income statement (trading accounts) for the provision for unrealised profit for the year ended 31 December 2007.

Donna has said that gross profit has improved since she started to transfer goods from her manufacturing account to the trading account at cost plus 30%. 'I am now earning two lots of gross profit', she tells you.

However, one of her managers says that he cannot see the point of marking up the goods to be transferred and he suggests that she discontinue the practice.

Required

(c)   Advise Donna on whether or not she should continue to transfer goods from her factory at cost plus 30%.

10   Marginal costing

In this chapter you will learn how to:

- explain the terms marginal cost, direct cost, indirect cost, variable cost, semi-variable cost, fixed cost, contribution, break-even and margin of safety

- calculate a break-even point using the appropriate formula, and represent it on a graph

- explain the limitations of break-even analysis

- identify the uses and limitations of marginal costing

- select and apply relevant techniques using marginal costing to aid decision making.

Key terms

Marginal cost: the cost of one extra unit.

Direct cost: is identified with the cost unit. Costs attributable to a particular product, e.g. direct materials and direct labour.

Variable cost: these costs vary with the level of production.

Indirect cost: this cost is not identified with the cost unit. Costs which cannot be attributed to a particular product, e.g. indirect labour such as the wages of supervisory staff.

Fixed cost: these costs do not vary with the level of production.

Semi-variable costs: these costs are partly fixed and partly variable.

In Chapter 9 you gained an understanding of how to record the costs associated with a manufacturing process. But how are these costs calculated? Do costs all behave the same way? What information can costs give us? These questions lead us into the realm of management and cost accounting rather than financial accounting. Financial accounting deals purely with the recording of historical data whereas management and cost accounting deals with the information that will form the basis of decision-making and cost control for both the present day and the future. This chapter will introduce you to one of the methods used within cost accounting, namely marginal costing.

Case study

Stanley Harold Ltd

Stanley Harold Ltd manufactures golf balls and sells to an international market. The golf balls are sold in box sets of 6.

Marginal costing

Marginal costing is a costing method which only considers **marginal costs**, which are those costs that are incurred when one extra unit is produced, for example the direct costs. **Direct costs** are those costs which can be identified with the actual production unit: namely the cost of direct material, cost of direct labour and any other **variable cost** which increases as production increases. **Indirect costs** are those costs which cannot be identified with the actual production unit and are not considered, for example staff administration costs.

The marginal costing method is used when:

- calculating the break-even point for a product
- considering whether to make or buy a product
- calculating the cost of a special order
- a business has a limiting factor which restricts its activities.

Types of costs

Within the marginal costing model it is important to distinguish between the different types of costs, as **fixed costs** are not considered.

- Variable costs: These costs vary in direct proportion with the level of production, for example direct wages and materials.
- Fixed costs: These costs do not vary in direct proportion to the level of production, for example rent payable, supervisors salaries and insurance.
- **Semi-variable costs**: These costs are partly fixed and partly variable, for example telephone costs which have a fixed line rental but a variable call charge cost.

Illustration

How to apply the correct cost behaviour

Stanley Harold Ltd has provided the following information for the year ended 31 January 2009.

- During the year 60,000 sets of golf balls were produced.

- Each set of golf balls uses £4 worth of materials. The material suppliers allowed a cash discount of 5% if Stanley Harold Ltd paid early. Only 25% of materials were paid for taking advantage of this discount. Material is a variable cost.

- Labour is paid for at a rate of £8 per hour. Unfortunately during the year orders could not be completed in normal working hours due to staff sickness. The directors of Stanley Harold Ltd agreed to pay overtime to workers so orders could be completed. The overtime was paid on 5,000 sets of golf balls at a rate of £14 per hour. Each set of golf balls takes 15 minutes to make. Labour is a variable cost.

- All other manufacturing costs were fixed and amounted to £298,125 for the year.

The manufacturing cost for the 60,000 sets of golf balls is therefore as follows.

	£
Material costs:	
With discount: 25% × 60,000 × (£4 × 0.95)	57,000
Without discount: 75% × 60,000 × £4	180,000
Labour costs:	
Overtime: 5,000 × (£14 × 0.25)	17,500
Without overtime: 55,000 × (£8 × 0.25)	110,000
Total variable costs	364,500
Fixed manufacturing costs	298,125
Total costs	662,625

Fig. 10.1 *Manufacturing cost*

From this illustration it is possible to further calculate useful costs; for example the total manufacturing cost per golf ball set is

$$\frac{£662,625}{60,000} = £11.04375$$

Whereas the variable cost per golf ball can be calculated as

$$\frac{£364,500}{60,000} = £6.075$$

The fixed cost per golf ball set can therefore be calculated as

$$\frac{£298,125}{60,000} = £4.96875$$

Activity

1. List five examples of each type of cost: variable, fixed and semi-variable.

Explanatory notes

- Layout: The layout clearly distinguishes between variable and fixed costs. The variable costs are made up of materials and labour.

- Material costs: In order to make the calculations easier the material costs at full price are shown separately to those with a discount. This method is recommended for examination questions.

- Labour costs: Once again in order to make calculations easier the labour costs are split between those with overtime and those without and at normal rates.

Contribution

The calculation of contribution is an important part of marginal costing as it identifies the amount of money made per unit towards covering fixed costs and profit. Once the fixed costs are covered, profit is made. **Contribution** is calculated as the difference between selling price per unit and variable cost per unit.

■ Illustration

How to apply contribution

Stanley Harold Ltd sells each golf ball set for £18. The variable cost is £6.075 and the early fixed costs are £298,125.

The contribution is therefore

selling price £18.00 less variable cost £6.075 = contribution £11.925

If 60,000 golf ball sets were sold in the year, a statement can be drawn up to show the total contribution and profit for the year.

Statement to show total contribution and profit for Stanley Harold Ltd for the year ended 31 January 2009

	£
Revenue (sales) (60,000 × £18)	1,080,000
Variable costs (60,000 × £6.075)	(364,500)
Total contribution	715,500
Fixed costs	298,125
Profit for the year	417,375

Fig. 10.2 *Statement to show total contribution and profit*

■ Explanatory note

The calculation for the total contribution can be checked as it is the total units sold times the contribution per unit. In this illustration it would be

60,000 × £11.925 = £715,500

AQA Examiner's tip

When asked to provide the formula for break-even ensure that a complete formula is given including contribution *per unit*.

Break-even analysis

One of the marginal costing techniques is break-even analysis, which identifies the level of output necessary to make neither a profit nor a loss. The break-even point is where total revenue equals total costs.

The number of units required to be sold at the break-even point is calculated using the formula:

$$\frac{\text{total fixed costs}}{\text{contribution per unit}}$$

At the **break-even point**, total revenue equals total cost. There are two methods of calculating this amount:

1 break-even in units × selling price

2 contribution to revenue (sales):

$$\frac{\text{total fixed costs}}{\text{total contribution/revenue (sales)}}$$

Illustration

How to apply a formula to calculate the break-even point

Using information from the previous illustration for Stanley Harold Ltd:

- the selling price for each golf ball set is £18
- the variable cost per set is £6.075
- the fixed costs for the year are £298,125.

The break-even point is therefore

$$\frac{\text{fixed costs}}{\text{contribution per unit}} = \frac{£298,125}{£11.925} = 25,000 \text{ golf ball sets}$$

The revenue at break-even is the same as total costs. In the above example this can therefore be calculated as

break-even in units × selling price = 25,000 × £18 = £450,000.

Alternatively, using the contribution to revenue (sales) method,

$$\frac{\text{fixed costs}}{\text{contribution per unit/selling price per unit}} = \frac{£298,125}{£11.925/£18} = £450,000$$

Margin of safety

The **margin of safety** is the amount of units between the amount of revenue (sales) made and the amount needed to break-even, where the amount of revenue (sales) exceeds the break-even point.

In the previous example Stanley Harold Ltd has a margin of safety of 60,000 − 25,000 = 35,000 golf ball sets. This means that it is making profit on the sales of 35,000 golf ball sets, namely 58.33% of its total revenue (sales). The rest is used to cover the fixed costs.

Target profit

The break-even formula can also be slightly amended to find the units required to be sold to achieve a specified target profit:

$$\frac{\text{total fixed costs} + \text{target profit}}{\text{contribution per unit}}$$

> **Key term**
>
> **Margin of safety:** the difference between the number of sales units achieved (or maximum output) and the number of units at the break-even point, where the amount of revenue (sales) achieved must exceed the break-even point otherwise a loss is made.

Illustration

How to calculate the units that need to be sold to achieve a target profit

The directors of Stanley Harold Ltd wish to achieve a target profit level of £35,775.

The golf sets they would have to produce and sell would therefore be

$$\frac{\text{total fixed costs} + \text{target profit}}{\text{contribution per unit}} = \frac{£298,125 + £35,775}{£11.925} = 28,000 \text{ golf sets}$$

Break-even chart

This information can all be represented on a break-even chart. A diagram showing where budgeted production exceeds the break-even point and so profit is made.

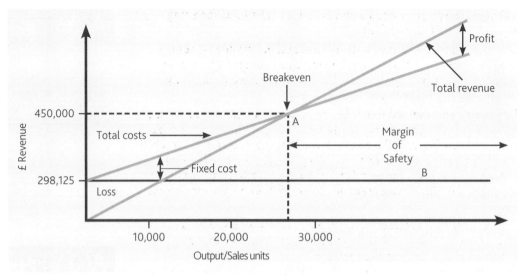

Fig. 10.3 *Break-even chart*

To draw a break-even chart the steps are as follows:

1 Label the axes clearly.

2 Calculate the break-even point using the formula:

$$\frac{\text{total fixed costs}}{\text{contribution per unit}}$$

3 Calculate the break-even point in revenue using the formula:

break – even point in units × selling price per unit

4 Plot the break-even point on the chart (point A). Try to ensure that the break-even sales units and sales revenue are in the middle of the chart.

5 Draw the fixed costs line across the chart as a horizontal line.

6 Draw the sale revenue line starting from (0,0) and going through the break-even point (point A).

7 Draw the total cost line starting from the point where the fixed cost line crosses the y-axis and going through the break-even point (point A).

8 Complete the chart by identifying the profit and loss areas and the margin of safety (line B).

The chart can be used to graphically illustrate:

■ the break-even point where total costs cross total revenues

■ the margin of safety being the difference between the break-even point and the maximum output production level; this is usually expressed in units

■ profit or loss at various production levels being the difference between the total costs and the total revenues lines at different production levels.

Limitations of break-even analysis

There are various limitations of break-even analysis:

■ It assumes that there are no changes in the levels of inventory (stock) so everything produced during that period is assumed to have been sold. This is unrealistic as most businesses have changing levels of inventory (stock) throughout the financial year.

Activity

2 Draw a break-even chart with the following information:

■ selling price of £40 per unit

■ variable cost of £25 per unit

■ fixed costs of £60,000 per year.

Identify the break-even point, the areas of profit and loss and the margin of safety.

- It does not allow product mix and is usually calculated for a single product, which is not realistic.
- Cost behaviour is assumed to be either fixed or variable, so semi-variable costs are not considered. Again this is unrealistic as many costs have behaviour that is not either perfectly fixed or perfectly variable but a combination of the two.
- Fixed costs are assumed to remain fixed for the whole period of time, so stepped fixed costs are not considered. Stepped fixed costs are costs which remain fixed until a certain level of business activity is reached when they increase in increments. They will remain fixed at this new increment until the next level of business activity. For example an increase in the storage costs due to an increase in the production level.
- Variable costs are assumed to be perfectly linear with the level of production, so changes in costs are not considered, for example overtime or bulk-buying discounts.
- The selling price is assumed to remain fixed throughout the year, so seasonal sales or discounts are again not considered.

Applying marginal costing in decision-making situations

Marginal costing can be used in a variety of business situations:

- whether to make or buy the products
- whether to accept a special order
- how to maximise profits where there are limited resources available.

Make or buy situations

One of the most common business decisions is whether a business should continue to manufacture the products themselves or whether to buy the products in from a supplier. Often the business is faced with a choice of satisfying customer demand with inventory (stock) bought in as it is unable to produce the goods required itself. On a purely financial basis the decision whether to make or buy in should be based on whether a positive contribution is made.

Illustration

How to reach make-or-buy decisions

Stanley Harold Ltd has six machines which are used in the manufacture of the golf ball sets. One of the machines has broken down and will take 4 weeks to repair. While the machine is being repaired the directors can lease a replacement machine which would cost £3,000 per week. The staff will need to be trained at a cost of £4,000 to use the machine, which would reduce production in that week from 5,000 golf ball sets to 4,000. Alternatively the directors can buy the golf ball sets in from a competitor at cost of £8 per set. The company would be able to buy 5,000 a week but would also have to pay a fixed delivery cost of £1,275.

The profit for this machine under both options for the 4 weeks would be as shown below.

- The procedure is to again identify the behaviour of each cost and revenue, that is to identify whether a cost varies with the level of production or does not vary with production and is therefore fixed. In this illustration the revenue (sales), variable costs of materials and labour and buy-in costs are variable. The lease, training costs and delivery costs are fixed.

- The illustration shows that the business makes more profit from manufacturing the golf sets themselves despite the extra lease and training costs and reduction in revenue (sales). The recommended action would be to continue to manufacture the golf ball sets themselves in order to maximise profit.

	To manufacture	To buy in
	£	£
Revenue (sales):		
To manufacture (4,000 × 1 wk + 5,000 × 3 wks) × £18	342,000	
To buy in (5,000 × 4 wks) × £18		360,000
Variable costs (4,000 × 1 + 5,000 × 3) × £6.075	(115,425)	
Buy-in cost (5,000 × 4) × £8		(160,000)
Lease (4 × £3,000)	(12,000)	
Delivery costs		(1,275)
Training costs	(4,000)	
Profit	210,575	198,725

Fig. 10.4 *Profit*

Special orders

Before accepting a special order the business must consider both the financial and non-financial factors. Financially it is important as to whether the order provides a positive contribution or not. But non-financial factors are important too, for example whether the order will lead to further orders and expand their share of the market, whether spare capacity is being utilised, will staff have to be retrained to make the product and will they wish to be retrained, will machinery have to be adapted if the specification of the product has been changed, how reliable is the customer, and how much disruption to the normal trading of the business will take place?

Illustration

How to evaluate a special order

Stanley Harold Ltd currently manufactures 60,000 golf ball sets a year but has spare capacity. The company receives a new order for 500 golf ball sets at £12 per set. The customer is based overseas in a new market area. There will be extra packaging costs for the order of £512.50, which is £1.025 per golf set.

The contribution for each golf set in the new order is shown below.

	£
Selling price	12.00
Variable manufacturing costs	(6.075)
Extra packaging costs	(1.025)
Contribution	4.90

Fig. 10.5 *Contribution*

Although this contribution is lower than the usual contribution of £11.925, the new order does make a positive contribution. The business has already passed the break-even point and is producing more units than is required for the target profit. It has spare capacity and therefore any extra contribution will be pure profit.

The total profit from this order will therefore be 500 × £4.90 = £2,450.

The non-financial factors should also be considered, namely that the order has been received from a new customer in a new overseas market area which will expand Stanley Harold Ltd's customer base. However, how reliable is this new customer? Can they guarantee that the new customer will pay on time? Also how easy will the distribution of the products be to the new customer?

Once these factors have been considered to the satisfaction of the business managers then the order should be accepted as it will increase profit as there is a positive contribution.

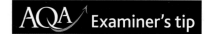

AQA Examiner's tip

When making a decision on whether to recommend acceptance of a special order candidates should consider both the financial and non-financial factors to give a balanced answer. Then a judgement should be made which can be for or against as long as it is justified.

Limiting factors

A business will often manufacture multiple products but have limited resources available to do so, for example limited labour hours or limited machine hours. An optimum production plan has to be devised in order to maximise profit with the resources available.

The process is as follows.

1 Calculate the contribution per unit.
2 Calculate the contribution per limiting factor, for example per labour hour.
3 Rank the products in order of the product with the highest contribution per limiting factor down to the product with the lowest.
4 Devise a production plan to maximise profits using the rank order.

Illustration

How to devise an optimum production plan

The directors of Stanley Harold Ltd decide to introduce a new product. They intend to manufacture and sell boxes of golf tees.

Information on their two products are as follows.

Table 1 *Information*

	Box of golf tees	Set of golf balls
Selling price	£6	£18
Labour	10 minutes at £3.60 per hour	30 minutes at £8.00 per hour
Materials	£2	£2.075
Expected demand for the following year	24,000 boxes	60,000 sets

The company only has 32,000 hours available and wishes to maximise profits by devising an optimum production plan.

■ The contribution per unit (selling price per unit less variable cost per unit) is

box of golf tees: £6 – £2.60 = £3.40
set of golf balls: £18 – £6.075 = £11.925

■ The contribution per limiting factor (contribution per unit divided by proportion of labour hours per unit) is

box of golf tees:
$$\frac{£3.40}{^1/_6} = £20.40$$

set of golf balls:
$$\frac{£11.925}{^1/_2} = £23.85$$

■ The rank order based on the highest contribution per limiting factor is therefore

set of golf balls: number 1
box of golf tees: number 2

■ The optimum production plan to maximise profit is therefore as follows.

Explanatory note

The amount of boxes of golf tees to be produced is based on the amount of remaining hours. There are 2,000 hours remaining. Each box takes 10 minutes to produce, and there are 60 minutes in an hour so six boxes can be produced in one hour, making a final calculation of 2,000 hours × 6 = 12,000 boxes.

Table 2 *Plan*

	Units	Hours
Sets of golf balls (expected demand)	60,000 sets requiring 30 minutes per box	30,000
Boxes of golf tees (remaining hours)	12,000 boxes requiring 10 minutes per set	2,000

In this chapter you will have learnt:

■ how to explain the method of marginal costing

■ how to explain the cost behaviour of direct costs, indirect costs, variable costs, fixed costs and semi-variable costs

■ how to explain the terms contribution and break-even

■ how to calculate the break-even point in units and revenue using the formulae

■ how to represent the break-even point on a chart

■ how to explain the limitations of break-even analysis

■ how to select and apply marginal-costing techniques for decision-making on make or buy decisions, special orders, and the maximisation of profit by finding the optimum production plan with a limiting factor.

1   Distinguish between fixed costs and variable costs. Give three examples of each.

2   AQA 2005 Jun ACC4 Q1
     The following break-even graph relates to Bungay Books Ltd for the year ending 31 December 2004.

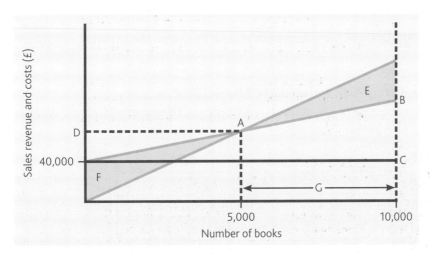

The selling price is £15 per book.

Required

(a)   Identify each of the following shown in the graph.
       A
       Line B
       Line C
       D
       Area E
       Area F
       G.

(b)   Calculate the value indicated at point D on the graph.

(c)   Calculate the marginal cost per unit.

(d)   Calculate the contribution per unit.

3   AQA 2003 Jan ACC7 Q1

The managers of Kerry Kent Ltd base their profit margin on the following formula: contribution per unit × 50%.

The company has received an order for 20 units of product 104A and wishes to make a profit of £16 per unit.

The expected costs for the total order are as follows.

	£
Direct materials	300
Direct labour	100

Present a detailed calculation of the selling price of each unit of product 104A.

4   AQA 2002 Jun ACC7 Q2

Donaldson Ltd manufactures only two products, Alto and Bass.

At present, the factory has one machine which is operating at 100% capacity. Only 520,000 labour hours are available in the year.

The cost per unit is as follows.

	Alto	Bass
Direct materials	10 metres at £5 per metre	20 metres at £5 per metre
Direct labour	44 hours at £5 per hour	32 hours at £5 per hour

The fixed costs for the year are £440,000.

The selling prices for one unit of Alto and Bass are £390 and £350 respectively.

Revenue (sales) in units for the year are as follows.

	Alto	Bass
Donaldson's revenue (sales) (units)	18,000	8,000
Competitor's revenue (sales) (units)	12,000	12,000
Total revenue (sales) (units)	30,000	20,000

Required

(a)   Calculate the contribution per unit for each product.

(b)   i Calculate the contribution per labour hour per unit for each product.

       ii State the optimum production plan which Donaldson Ltd could introduce which would maximise profit.

(c)   Assess the effects this new production plan would have on the manufacturing companies in competition with Donaldson Ltd.

5   AQA 2004 Jun ACC4 Q1

Ron owns a business that manufactures kettles at a marginal cost of £18 each.

The selling price is £22.50 per kettle.

The fixed costs are currently £90,000 per annum.

Required

(a)   Explain the term 'marginal cost'. Give an example.

(b)   Calculate the total contribution if 25,000 kettles are sold.

(c)   Identify the formula used to calculate the profit for the year (net profit) margin.

(d)   Calculate the profit for the year (net profit) to sales margin if 25,000 kettles are sold.

(e)   Calculate how many extra kettles will need to be sold if the fixed costs increase next year by 20%.

(f)   Calculate the selling price per kettle if the same profit for the year (net profit) margin is required after the increase in fixed costs. (Assume that 25,000 kettles will be sold.)

(g)   Draft a memorandum addressed to Ron explaining one advantage and one disadvantage of using a graph to present a break-even point.

> **■ Link**
>
> For further information on the profit for the year (net profit) margin, see *AQA AS Accounting*, Chapter 9.

6   AQA 2008 Jan ACC4 Q1

Sid owns a business in a seaside resort. He sells greetings cards.

On average each card costs 50p to buy and is sold for £1.20.

The annual business fixed costs are £110,000.

Sid has set a target profit for the year of £30,000.

Required

(a)   Calculate the contribution per greetings card.

(b)   Calculate the number of greetings cards which Sid needs to sell to achieve the target profit of £30,000. State the formula used.

Unfortunately, Sid's supplier decides to increase the cost of the greetings cards by 30%.

Required

(c)   Calculate the number of *extra* greetings cards which Sid would need to sell to maintain a target profit of £30,000 following the increase in cost per card.

Sid does not believe that the business can sell the *extra* greetings cards in the seaside resort.

Required

(d)   Advise Sid of *two* methods by which the business could maintain profit levels without selling the extra greetings cards.

7   Cilin Ltd manufactures two products, the Qi and the Xi.

The Qi currently has a selling price of £20 per unit and it costs £15 to manufacture.

The Xi is selling well.

The economic climate has led to a decrease in the number of units of Qi sold and the financial manager of Cilin Ltd is unsure whether to reduce the selling price down to £18 to try to meet competitors' prices or whether to buy the products in, partly completed. These products could be bought in at a cost of £12 each and each unit would need to be completed at an extra cost of £3. Unfortunately these products have a lower quality than the ones produced by Cilin Ltd and if purchased over 40% of the workforce would need to be made redundant.

Discuss whether Cilin Ltd should make or buy in the product Qi.

11 Absorption costing

In this chapter you will learn how to:

- explain the term absorption costing
- calculate profit using absorption costing
- explain the term cost centre
- allocate and apportion costs
- calculate overhead absorption rates
- apply overhead absorption rates
- apply concepts to pricing policy
- cost a simple project.

Key terms

Cost unit: a unit of production or service which absorbs the cost centre's overheads costs, for example, a product such as a television set or a service such as a restaurant meal.

Allocation: the process of charging costs which derive from a cost centre directly to that particular cost centre.

Apportionment: the process of charging overhead costs to a cost centre on a rational basis.

Cost centre: a production or service location whose costs may be attributed to cost units, for example, a production department.

Production department: where the product is actually made, for example, the machining department.

Labour intensive: the production or service location has more direct labour hours than machine hours.

In the previous chapter you were introduced to one of the most commonly used methods in cost accounting, namely marginal costing. However this method is often compared to the use of another method of cost accounting, namely absorption costing. The main difference between the two is the treatment of fixed costs, which is covered within this chapter. Do not dismiss either method as both methods have their own uses and limitations.

Case study

Maureen Rose plc

Maureen Rose plc manufactures bags. The company has one factory. There are two production departments: cutting and finishing, and two service departments: maintenance and canteen.

Absorption costing

Absorption costing absorbs the factory overheads into the total production cost for each **cost unit** produced in a factory. Whereas marginal costing only considers the variable costs, absorption costing considers all production costs including fixed and variable overheads.

The process of absorption occurs when all production overheads are **allocated** and **apportioned** to a **cost centre**, which is a location such as a **production department**. The total is then absorbed into a cost unit, such as a product or service, using an overhead absorption rate (OAR).

The methods of absorption include:

- direct labour hour rate
- direct machine hour rate.

The basis selected is based on which factor most influences the overhead, for example if the production department uses mostly labour hours it is described as **labour intensive** and the direct labour hour rate is chosen. If the production department uses mostly machine hours it is described as either **machine intensive** or capital intensive and the direct machine hour rate is chosen.

Calculation of the overhead absorption rate (OAR)

The stages used to calculate the overhead absorption rate are as follows.

1 Distinguish between production departments, for example a cutting department, and service departments, for example the canteen.
2 Decide on the correct bases to be used to apportion the overheads between the departments, for example according to the percentage of the total floor space for the cutting department and the proportion of employees working in the department for the canteen.

Machine intensive: the production or service location has more direct machine hours than labour hours. The location can otherwise be known as capital-intensive.

Service department: these departments support the other departments, for example technical support and canteen.

Activities

1 List five possible **service departments** which a large manufacturing public limited company could have.

2 List five possible service departments which a school or college could have.

3 Draw up a schedule to apportion the overheads between all of the departments.

4 Complete the schedule by apportioning the total of the overheads of each service department to each of the production departments.

5 Total up the overheads for each production department.

6 Divide the total for each department by the correct basis, for example labour hours or machine hours depending on whether the department is labour intensive or machine intensive, to give the overhead absorption rate (OAR) for each production department.

Stages 1–5

Illustration

How to apportion overheads using the elimination method, or simplified method

The following information is available for Maureen Rose plc for the year ended 31 October 2008.

Information available for Maureen Rose plc for the year ended 31 October 2008

	£
Overheads:	
Buildings insurance	50,000
Heating and lighting	70,000
Machine insurance	100,000
Rent	120,000
Cutting supervisor	37,100
Finishing supervisors	76,900

Fig. 11.1 *Information*

Additional information:

Table 1 *Additional information*

	Cutting department	Finishing department	Maintenance	Canteen
Floor area, m²	50,000	30,000	15,000	5,000
Machine net book value	£150,000	£450,000	–	–

The service departments are apportioned to the production departments on the following basis.

Table 2 *Service department apportionment*

	Cutting department	Finishing department	Maintenance	Canteen
	%	%	%	%
Canteen	50	40	10	–
Maintenance	75	25	–	–

The overhead apportionment schedule would therefore appear as follows.

Overhead apportionment schedule for Maureen Rose plc

Overhead	Basis	Cutting	Finishing	Maintenance	Canteen
		£	£	£	£
Cutting supervisor	Direct	37,100	–	–	–
Finishing supervisors	Direct	–	76,900	–	–
Buildings insurance	Floor area	25,000	15,000	7,500	2,500
Heating and lighting	Floor area	35,000	21,000	10,500	3,500
Machine insurance	Machine NBV	25,000	75,000	–	–
Rent	Floor area	60,000	36,000	18,000	6,000
		182,100	223,900	36,000	12,000
Canteen	(50%:40%:10%)	6,000	4,800	1,200	(12,000)
Maintenance	(75%:25%)	27,900	9,300	(37,200)	–
		216,000	238,000	–	–

Fig. 11.2 *Overhead apportionment schedule*

Explanatory notes

■ Bases of apportionment: The basis to be used to apportion the overheads is easily identified as it is usually the most realistic, for example, insurance. The most equitable way to apportion the building insurance overhead is by the proportion of floor space held by each department whereas a better way to apportion the machine insurance is according to the proportion of the total machine net book value. Given the information available the most realistic basis to be used for the heating and lighting and rent is the proportion of the total floor space in both instances.

■ Apportionment of the service departments: The most important thing to recognise is whether there is any interdependency between the service departments. In this case both service departments support the production departments but the canteen also supports the maintenance department. Once this has been identified then this service department must be apportioned first to both the production departments and the other service department.

AQA Examiner's tip

When there is interdependency between the service departments remember to include the first service department apportionment in the second service department apportionment. In the above example remember to include the 10% of the canteen costs in the apportionment of the total maintenance costs.

The elimination method of apportioning the reciprocal service departments' overheads is quick as each service department has its overheads apportioned only once to the other departments. However if the service department which has any apportionment to the other service department is not apportioned first, the continuous allotment method will result whereby there is no preferred order to the apportionment, and so the apportionment continues until the balance in each service department is zero. This is not the recommended method for the examinations due to time constraints.

■ Illustration

How to apportion overheads using the continous allotment method, or repeated distribution method

Using the information from the previous illustration, we would have the following overhead apportionment schedule.

Overhead	Basis	Cutting	Finishing	Maintenance	Canteen
		£	£	£	£
b/fwd		182,100	223,900	36,000	12,000
Maintenance	(75%:25%)	27,000	9,000	(36,000)	–
Canteen	(50%:40%:10%)	6,000	4,800	1,200	(12,000)
Maintenance	(75%:25%)	900	300	(1,200)	–
		216,000	238,000	–	–

Fig. 11.3 *Overhead apportionment schedule*

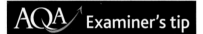 Examiner's tip

Make sure that the schedule is clearly laid out with each part of the process clearly shown as marks are allocated for each stage.

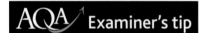 Examiner's tip

Ensure that the basis used for each overhead is clearly identified as there are usually marks in the examination for doing this.

As can be seen, the same final answer is achieved but the process is longer. This can be a repetitive process if each department apportions their overheads to each other repeatedly.

■ Activity

3 List five different overheads and state a reasonable basis for each one which could be used to apportion the overhead to the different production departments.

Stage 6

■ Illustration

How to calculate the overhead absorption rate (OAR)

The directors of Maureen Rose plc absorb their overheads on the following basis:

■ The cutting department uses more direct machine hours than direct labour hours. It is therefore machine or capital intensive and overheads are absorbed using direct machine hours.

■ The finishing department uses more direct labour hours than direct machine hours. It is therefore labour intensive and overheads are absorbed using direct labour hours.

The overheads for the year ended 31 October 2008 were:

■ cutting department: £216,000
■ finishing department: £238,000.

The cutting department has 12,000 machine hours and the finishing department has 14,000 labour hours.

The **overhead aborption rate (OAR)** is the rate at which the overheads are absorbed into the cost unit. It is calculated as

$$\frac{\text{department overhead in pounds}}{\text{department direct machine hours or direct labour hours}}$$

The overhead absorption rate for the cutting department is therefore

$$\frac{\pounds216,000}{\pounds12,000} = \pounds18.00 \text{ per machine hour}$$

The overhead absorption rate for the finishing department is therefore

$$\frac{\pounds238,000}{14,000} = \pounds17.00 \text{ per labour hour}$$

Use of the overhead absorption rate (OAR)

Once the OAR has been calculated it is possible to calculate the **full cost** of a cost unit.

▋ Illustration

How to calculate the full cost of a cost unit

Maureen Rose plc has the following information:

- Each bag takes 30 minutes of machine time in the cutting department and 2 hours of labour in the finishing department, at £8 per hour, to manufacture.
- Each bag uses 0.5 metres of material at £22 per metre.

The full cost per bag is therefore as shown below.

	£
Materials (0.5 metres x £22 per metre)	11.00
Labour (2 hours x £8 per hour)	16.00
Cutting department overheads (£18.00 per machine hour x 0.5 hours)	9.00
Finishing department overheads (£17.00 per labour hour x 2 hours)	34.00
Full cost	70.00

Fig. 11.4 *Cost per bag*

▋ Explanatory note

The total production or full cost can now be calculated by absorbing the overheads according to the amount of machine hours and labour hours used by the cost unit and adding them to the direct costs. Each OAR is applied separately.

Explanatory note

The total production or full cost of producing one bag is therefore £70. This includes the direct costs and an apportionment of the overheads for each bag. It is important to appreciate that this method gives only an approximate estimate of what the product actually cost, for example how realistic is it to absorb a production department's overheads either on machine hours or labour hours especially if that department is not strongly capital intensive or labour intensive? There is also the issue of the arbitrary method of apportioning the service departments' overheads and the rounding throughout. This is especially important to understand when using the pricing strategy 'full cost plus' to obtain a selling price for the future.

■ Key terms

Under-absorption: occurs when fewer units are produced than was predicted in the budget and therefore not all the overheads are absorbed into the cost unit.

Over-absorption: occurs when more units are produced than was predicted in the budget and therefore more overheads are absorbed into the cost unit.

Pricing strategies

Companies often base their pricing strategy on the budgeted full cost of a cost unit.

For example if the directors of Maureen Rose plc expect next year's costs to be identical to this year's and also wish to use the pricing strategy, budgeted full cost + 20%, the selling price for the next period would be £70.00 × 1.2 = £84.00.

This naturally assumes that budgeted costs are realistic estimations of the future actual costs.

The profit from each cost unit sold is, therefore, £14.

Under-absorption or over-absorption

Absorption rates are often calculated on budgeted costs and production levels at the start of the year. This can lead to problems when actual costs and volumes of production are not the same as those budgeted, leading to an **under-absorption** or **over-absorption** of costs. The difference between the budgeted overheads and the actual overheads is recorded as an adjustment within the profit and loss account. Under-absorption is when fewer units are produced than was predicted which means that not all costs have been passed onto the cost unit and therefore profit is less, whereas over-absorption is when more units are produced which means that more costs have been passed onto the cost unit and therefore profit is more.

In this chapter you will have learnt:

- how to explain absorption costing to distinguish it from marginal costing
- how to distinguish between a cost centre and a cost unit
- how to allocate, apportion and absorb overheads using the absorption rate
- how to apply the absorption rates to work out the full cost of a cost unit, and from there to work out the selling price of a product.

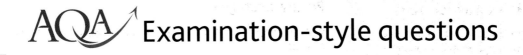

AQA Examination-style questions

1   Explain the terms
   a)   cost centre
   b)   cost unit.

2   Distinguish between the terms allocation, apportion and absorption.

3   AQA 2002 Jun ACC7 Q4
   The following information relates to the production departments of Springson Ltd.

	Cutting department	Machining department
Direct machine hours, h	4,000	33,000
Direct labour hours, h	30,000	20,000
Cost of machinery, £	20,000	260,000
Floor area, m²	9,000	21,000

   The factory overheads for the year ended 31 March 2002 were as follows.

	£
Machinery insurance	28,000
Rent	12,000
Depreciation	56,000
Light and heat	18,000

   Required
   (a)   Prepare an overhead apportionment schedule apportioning the factory overheads to the appropriate departments.
   (b)   Calculate the overhead absorption rates for each production department. State the bases used and give one reason for your choice.

4   AQA 2008 Jun ACC7 Q3 a–d
   Jameson Ltd manufactures one product. The following information relates to the two production and two service departments for one four-week period.

	Production departments		Service departments	
	Machining	Assembly	Maintenance	Canteen
Overheads	£143,500	£154,700	£165,800	£176,900
Direct machine hours	18,845	14,050	–	–
Direct labour hours	6,065	20,350	–	–

The service departments' overheads are apportioned to the production departments on the following basis:

	Machining	Assembly	Canteen
Maintenance	60%	30%	10%
Canteen	40%	60%	

Required

(a) Prepare an overhead apportionment schedule apportioning the service departments' overheads to the appropriate departments for one period.

(b) Calculate the overhead absorption rates for each production department. State the bases used and give a reason for each choice.

The manager of Jameson Ltd calculates selling price per unit based on full cost plus a 25% mark-up.

The costs per unit are:

materials: 3 metres at £4 per metre

labour: 7 hours at £8 per hour.

Each unit takes 3 hours in the machining department and 4 hours in the assembly department. All overheads are fixed.

(c) Calculate the full cost per unit.

(d) Calculate the selling price per unit.

5   Compare the advantages of using absorption costing with the advantages of using marginal costing to set a selling price.

12 Activity based costing

In this chapter you will learn how to:

- explain the term activity based costing

- explain and compare the terms cost pools and cost drivers

- compare activity based costing with both marginal and absorption costing, identifying the uses, benefits and limitations of each.

In this chapter you will be introduced to one of the most up-to-date methods of cost accounting, namely Activity Based Costing (known as ABC). This method was revolutionary when it was first introduced as it focuses on the causes of costs and not their behaviour. Simply the most important consideration is not whether a cost is fixed or variable but rather what causes the cost to change.

This is a new topic to the accounting specification. Only prose questions will be set in the examination.

Case study

Einnoc Ltd

Einnoc Ltd uses activity based costing to cost its output. The company produces two products, Ein and Noc. Production of Ein is in large batches of 1,000 units, whereas production of Noc is in smaller batches of 200 units.

Key terms

Cost pool: the location of a group of related indirect costs.

Cost driver: the factors which cause costs of an activity and also cause these costs to change.

Activity based costing?

This method of costing was developed in the 1970s and 1980s as an alternative to absorption costing. An organisation's activities are analysed into groups of costs, one group for each major activity. These groups are called **cost pools**. Factors are then identified which cause the costs to change. These factors are called **cost drivers**. The cost of the output is then calculated according to the output's level of the activity.

A cost rate per activity is calculated as follows.

$$\frac{\text{cost pool}}{\text{cost driver}}$$

activity $\longrightarrow$ cost pool $\longrightarrow$ cost driver $\longrightarrow$ cost rate

Examples of cost pools and cost drivers

These are examples for a stores department (previously a service department under absorption costing).

Table 1 *Cost pools and cost drivers*

Activity	Cost pools	Cost drivers	Cost rate
Receiving goods into stores	Cost of receiving goods into the stores	Number of deliveries into stores	$\frac{\text{cost of receiving goods}}{\text{number of deliveries}}$
Setting up production equipment	Cost of setting up production equipment	Number of set-ups carried out	$\frac{\text{cost of setting up}}{\text{number of set-ups}}$
Student administration in a college	Cost of administration	Number of students	$\frac{\text{cost of administration}}{\text{number of students}}$
Issuing goods to production	Cost of issuing goods to production department	Number of requisitions from production department	$\frac{\text{cost of issuing goods}}{\text{number of requisitions}}$

Examiner's tip

In the examination, questions on activity based costing will not be set which require the calculation of the cost rate. An understanding of the terms and approach is, however, required.

Explanatory note

In the illustration the production run costs of one unit of Noc is five times that of one unit of Ein. This arose as the product Noc has fewer production runs than the product Ein. The cost of each product therefore varies according to the product's level of activity. This difference would not be identified using the absorption costing method where the cost of production runs is treated as part of general overheads.

It can therefore be seen that more activity causes more costs to be incurred. If an order requires six requisitions then six times the cost of issuing rate is allocated to that order. Activity based costing therefore directly links the activity with the costs.

Illustration

How to use activity based costing in the manufacturing sector

Einnoc Ltd has identified a major activity as the production runs of the factory machines. The cost pool associated with this activity in a financial year is expected to be £500,000. The cost driver of this activity is the number of runs, as the costs increase in direct proportion to this number. A batch of either product requires one production run. It is expected that there will be 50 production runs in the financial year.

The cost driver rate is £500,000/50 = £10,000 per production run.

Using this rate one unit of Ein would incur production run costs of £10,000/1,000 = £10 and one unit of Noc would incur production run costs of £10,000/200 = £50. These production run costs are then added to the other unit costs to calculate the total production cost per unit.

Comparisons between the different methods of costing

Table 2 Costing methods

	Marginal costing	Absorption costing	Activity based costing
Uses	For decision making, as it identifies the extra costs and revenues incurred by the production and sale of an additional unit, e.g. make or buy decisions, limiting factors.	For decision making, as it includes a portion of fixed costs into each cost unit, e.g. calculating the selling price using the pricing strategy 'full cost plus'.	For decision making, as it charges each product with an accurate cost based on its use of an activity. If the activity changes, the related effect on the cost can be assessed, so costs can be controlled. For example, how much will costs increase if there is an extra batch run?
Benefits	Easily understood and applied in decision making, being cost effective. Contribution is identified, which is useful, e.g., in make or buy decisions and where there are limiting factors such as limited labour hours.	All costs are considered, so a total production cost per unit is identified. The effect of an increase in any one cost can be assessed, whether it is direct or indirect.	Avoids apportioning overheads using a basis that may not be relevant, e.g. machine hours for administration costs. Batch sizes influence costs, which is ignored by absorption costing, e.g. set-up costs are more expensive for small production runs.
Limitations	Indirect and direct costs are both divided into either fixed or variable costs. Fixed costs are not allocated to cost centres and cost units, but are regarded as time-based and are linked to accounting periods rather than units of output.	The final basis used to calculate the overhead absorption rate may not be relevant for all the overheads in the production department. New technology has led to a reduction in the use of labour hours as a valid basis. If inventory (stock) levels decrease, absorption costing records a lower profit than absorption as costs from previous periods are set against income.	There are still cost pools that are not caused by one particular cost driver but by several, e.g. the cost of marketing is caused by the number of staff hours and the number of marketing campaigns.

Activity

1 Identify five business activities, their cost pools and a cost driver for each activity. Select at least two activities from the service sector.

In this chapter you will have learnt:

- the term 'activity based costing'

- how to explain and identify cost pools and cost drivers

- how to compare the uses of activity based costing against both marginal and absorption costing, while identifying the fact that each method has its own benefits and limitations.

AQA Examiner's tip

This new topic in the specification lends itself towards a prose question, especially on the content of the above table. It is recommended that this is learnt and remembered.

AQA Examination-style questions

1 Define the term activity based costing.

2 Explain the terms cost pool and cost driver. Give an example of each.

3 Define each of the following terms:
- activity based costing
- marginal costing
- absorption costing.

Give an example of when each would be used.

4 'Activity based costing was developed as an alternative to absorption costing.'
(a) Explain how activity based costing is used to calculate the cost of a product.
(b) Explain *two* benefits of using activity based costing as opposed to using absorption costing.

5 Cao plc produces a variety of products according to customer demand. Some products have had the same specification for many years whereas others are regularly updated to meet customer requirements. Some products have long production runs while others are produced in small batches for specific customers.

Write a memorandum to the financial director of Cao plc explaining whether marginal costing, absorption costing or activity based costing would be the most appropriate costing method for the company.

13 Standard costing and variance analysis

One of the major uses of any costing information is the evaluation of performance. Not only calculating how much each product has cost to make but also evaluating how much it **should** have cost to make. The first was discussed in the previous three chapters and now the last will be covered in this chapter, when we look at standard costing. Once a business has set standard or expected costs it can then compare them to actual costs and evaluate its performance either as a whole or department by department. Obviously if costs are more than they should have been then actions need to be taken so that the reasons behind these increased costs can be investigated, so profit is not reduced in the future. The same comparison can also be made between standard revenues and actual revenues. In this chapter you will be introduced to standard costing and the performance decisions which can be made using standard costs and revenues.

Topic 1   Standard costing

In this topic you will learn how to:

- explain the term standard costing
- explain how standard costs are determined
- evaluate standard costing.

Key terms

Standard costing: the preparation and use of standard costs, including the calculation of variances.

Standard cost: a predetermined cost which should be achieved through an efficient working environment.

Case study

Legin Ltd

Legin Ltd manufactures a single product, the Keza. For many years the financial director has maintained a standard costing system.

What is standard costing?

Standard costing is the preparation and use of costs which should be achieved with efficient working conditions and manufacturing performance. These costs ought to be achieved and are called **standard costs**. Standard costing involves the comparison of these predetermined standard costs with actual costs. Any difference between the actual and standard cost is called a variance, and should be investigated.

Illustration

How to calculate standard costs

The financial director of Legin Ltd has calculated the standard costs per unit of Keza as follows.

	£
Direct materials (4 metres at £5 per metre)	20.00
Direct labour (6 hours at £8 per hour)	48.00
Standard cost per unit	68.00

Fig. 13.1 *Standard cost card per unit of Keza*

The purposes of standard costing

Standard costing is frequently used within a manufacturing business as it provides detailed information to management which helps to establish why budgeted performance differs from actual performance.

Its many purposes include:

- assisting in budget setting and evaluating performance
- acting as a control device by highlighting those activities which are not performing as expected and may need investigation and corrective action.
- providing information on future costs for future decision-making
- providing a motivating target for employees to aim for
- providing an acceptable cost for valuing inventory (stock).

Setting standards

Standards must be achievable as they are a yardstick against which efficiency is measured. If based on ideal working conditions, where the workers and machines are working to optimum efficiency at all times, the standards will be demotivating as they will never be achieved. Similarly, if based on a basic fixed standard that has been in force for many years and can be easily achieved due to advances in technology, the standards can be equally demotivating. Therefore they should be a realistic target by allowing for eventualities such as staff sickness and machine breakdown.

- Standards are usually based on past performance. This is the most cost-effective method, but there may be past inefficiencies which would then be built into the future standards.
- Standards can also be set using engineering studies where workers are observed using time and motion studies. However, again these can be misleading as well as costly to establish as they take time to complete and workers may not give a realistic impression of their normal working performance as they may feel that they will be judged on it. Working too quickly would set too high standards which cannot be achieved and working too slowly may result in dismissal.

Sources of information for setting standards for direct costs

The following are examples of sources of information for setting standards for direct costs. It is not an exhaustive list.

Direct material

Amount of material used:

- observation of the manufacturing process
- records of historical amounts used
- technical data from the supplier on recommended amounts to be used
- product specification
- past data on the amount of wastage
- an assessment of the quality of the material to be used
- an assessment of the performance of the equipment and labour force available.

Explanatory note

The **standard cost card** on page 138 shows that each unit of Keza should use 4 metres of material which cost £5 per metre and 6 hours of labour which cost £8 per hour. In total £20 should be spent on material and £48 on labour.

Key term

Standard cost card: specifies the standard costs predetermined for one unit.

Cost of material:

- predicted currency exchange rates
- price list from suppliers including any bulk buying, trade or cash discounts available
- information on predicted inflation
- records of historical costs paid
- data on the effects on cost of anticipated seasonal variations/scarce availability.

Direct labour

Amount of labour time:

- an assessment of the training and skills of workforce
- an assessment of any changes in production processes
- observation of the workforce, for example by time and motion studies
- records of historical output and efficiency levels.

Cost of labour:

- data on current pay rates after considering grade of workforce used
- data on industry and local rates
- published legislation, for example on the minimum wage
- an assessment of any anticipated wage rises and bonuses
- an assessment of future overtime rates.

Advantages and disadvantages of standard costing

Advantages

- Predetermined standards make the preparation of forecasts and budgets much easier as the information has already been collected.
- Costs and revenues are controlled through the use of variances, that is the comparison of standard costs with actual results, which will highlight the efficiencies and inefficiencies within the business. Remedial actions can then be taken.
- The recording of inventory (stock) issues is simplified as they are all at standard cost.
- Both internal and external reports can then be produced from the standard costing bookkeeping system.
- Employees can be motivated to achieve targets which should result in better performance especially if rewards are given when targets are achieved or passed.

Disadvantages

- Standards have little use if set either too high or too low, and so must be regularly reviewed and reset.
- Standards are best used for businesses which have a well-established and repetitive process so that resetting of standards is kept to a minimum.
- Collecting the information to set a standard may be time-consuming and costly.
- In a rapidly changing technological economy the information may quickly become out of date.

Activity

1 List three different products in a new manufacturing business, in an established manufacturing business and in the service industry. Describe the different measures which would have to be taken to collate the necessary information needed to draw up the cost standards for each.

In this topic you will have learnt:

- the term standard costing
- how standard costs are predetermined
- the advantages and disadvantages of using standard costing.

1   Define the term standard cost.

2   Explain *two* advantages and *two* disadvantages of using standard costing to a manufacturing business.

3   Evaluate the different methods by which standards can be set.

Topic 2   Variance analysis

In this topic you will learn how to:

- calculate variances and sub-variances

- explain the significance of each variance and sub-variance, including interrelationships between variances

- explain how businesses use variances and sub-variances

- prepare statements reconciling budgeted profit with actual profit based on variances

- prepare statements reconciling budgeted costs with actual costs based on variances.

Key terms

Variance: the difference between a standard cosvt or revenue and an actual cost or revenue.

Favourable variance: the actual figures are better than the standard figures in the budget resulting in a higher actual profit than was expected.

Adverse variance: the actual figures are worse than the standard figures in the budget, resulting in a lower actual profit than was expected.

Cost variance: the difference between the standard cost and the actual cost.

What is variance analysis?

Variance analysis is the process of comparing actual costs and revenues with standard costs and revenues and investigating any reasons for the difference between them. Corrective action can then be taken by each budget manager. **Variances** are categorised into either a **favourable variance** or an **adverse variance**.

A favourable variance has a positive effect on profit, that is the actual costs are lower than the standard, or actual revenue is higher than the standard.

An adverse variance has a negative effect on profit, that is the actual costs are higher than the standard, or actual revenue is lower than the standard.

A manager will usually look into the possible causes of an adverse variance as this decreases profit. A favourable variance will increase profit, but if there is a large favourable variance it may still need to be investigated as it could be as a result of poor budget setting. Remember that if budgets are easily achieved they lose validity as targets.

Variances and sub-variances

The following variances are to be studied for the examination. (There are other variances which can be calculated but these are not considered within the current specification.)

- Material total **cost variance**: the difference between the standard expected cost and the actual cost of material.
- Labour total cost variance: the difference between the standard expected cost and the actual cost of labour.
- Sales total **revenue variance**: the difference between the standard revenue expected and the actual revenue received from revenue (sales).

Each total variance is broken down into two **sub-variances** so fuller analysis can be made of the reasons for the variance. Namely did the variance arise due to a difference in prices paid or due to a difference in the resources used?

- material total cost variance: price sub-variance and usage sub-variance
- labour total cost variance: rate sub-variance and efficiency sub-variance
- sales total revenue variance: price sub-variance and volume sub-variance.

Cost variances

■ Illustration

Why are cost variances needed?

Legin Ltd produces a single product, the Keza.

	£
Direct materials (4 metres at £5 per metre)	20.00
Direct labour (6 hours at £8 per hour)	48.00
Standard cost per unit	68.00

Fig. 13.2 *Standard cost card per unit of Keza*

The expected production is 4,000 units for month 1.

The actual costs for month 1 were as follows.

	£
Direct materials (3.5 metres at £6 per metre)	21.00
Direct labour (5 hours at £9 per hour)	45.00
Actual cost	66.00

Fig. 13.3 *Actual costs*

The actual production for month 1 was as expected.

■ Explanatory notes

- Direct materials: The actual direct material cost per unit for month 1 is £21 which is more than the standard cost per unit for month 1. But is this due to a change in the price of each metre or the usage of material?

- Direct labour: The actual direct labour cost per unit for month 1 is £45 which is less than the standard cost per unit for month 1. But is this due to a change in the hourly rate or the efficiency of the workforce?

- Total cost: The total actual cost is slightly less per unit, so overall profit will be higher than expected. But a full analysis is needed identifying the exact area of change and possible reasons for the change.

■ Illustration

How to calculate materials cost variance

The material total cost variance for Legin Ltd is as follows.

	£	
Standard cost (4000 × £20.00)	80,000	
Actual cost (4000 × £21.00)	84,000	
Total cost variance	4,000	adverse

Fig. 13.4 *Material cost variance*

Explanatory notes

■ This is an adverse variance as the actual cost is greater than the standard cost and so actual profit will be reduced by £4,000 compared to the budgeted profit.

■ There is no change in the number of units produced so is this difference due to paying a higher price per metre or because more metres of material were used for this particular month? Material sub-variances can be calculated to answer these questions.

Material price variance

The actual quantity of material used to produce 4,000 units was 3.5 metres × 4,000 = 14,000 metres.

	£	
Standard cost should have been (14,000 × £5)	70,000	
Actual cost was (14,000 × £6)	84,000	
Material price variance	14,000	adverse

Fig. 13.5 *Material price variance*

Material usage variance

The standard quantity of material used for 4,000 units was expected to be 4 metres × 4,000 = 16,000 metres.

	£	
Standard usage should have been (16,000 × £5)	80,000	
Actual usage was (14,000 × £5)	70,000	
Material usage variance	10,000	favourable

Fig. 13.6 *Material usage variance*

The calculations of the sub-variances can be checked:

£14,000 adverse − £10,000 favourable = £4,000 adverse total variance

Key terms

Material price variance: the difference between the actual price paid and the standard price expected to be paid, for the actual materials used.

Material usage variance: the difference between the actual materials used and the standard materials expected to be used, at the standard price paid.

AQA Examiner's tip

In the examination there are various acceptable ways in which to record the direction of the variance, for example a favourable variance which results in a higher revenue or a lower cost and so increases profit can be recorded as favourable, FAV or F variance, and an adverse variance which results in a lower revenue or a higher cost and so a decrease in profit can be recorded as adverse, ADV or A variance. +/– and brackets should be avoided.

Explanatory notes

■ It can therefore be seen the £4,000 adverse total variance is split between the two sub-variances.

■ The adverse price variance means that the company has paid more for the material than expected whereas the favourable usage variance results from using less material than was expected.

■ One possible reason for the variances could be that the material was of better quality, therefore it cost more, but less was used perhaps due to less wastage due to fewer flaws etc.

■ Of the two variances the adverse price variance should be investigated to see if the company can negotiate a cheaper price from the supplier or find an alternative supplier, whilst maintaining the same quality. However, it should also be checked as to whether the standard for material usage was incorrectly set as a large favourable variance has arisen. Did they overestimate the amount of material that would be needed per unit?

Illustration

How to calculate labour cost variance

The labour total cost variance for Legin Ltd is as follows.

	£	
Standard cost (4,000 × £48.00)	192,000	
Actual cost (4,000 × £45.00)	180,000	
Total cost variance	12,000	favourable

Fig. 13.7 *Labour cost variance*

Labour rate variance

The actual number of hours used to produce 4,000 units was 5 hours × 4,000 = 20,000 hours.

	£	
Standard cost should have been (20,000 × £8)	160,000	
Actual cost was (20,000 × £9)	180,000	
Labour rate variance	20,000	adverse

Fig. 13.8 *Labour rate variance*

Labour efficiency variance

The standard quantity of labour for 4,000 units was expected to be 6 hours × 4,000 = 24,000 hours.

	£	
Standard efficiency should have been (24,000 × £8)	192,000	
Actual efficiency was (20,000 × £8)	160,000	
Labour efficiency variance	32,000	favourable

Fig. 13.9 *Labour efficiency variance*

The calculations of the sub-variances can be checked:

£32,000 favourable – £20,000 adverse = £12,000 favourable total variance

Alternative method of variance calculation

Some students find it easier to calculate the sub-variances using formulae. This tends to be quicker.

Illustration

How to calculate variances using formulae

Using the information from the previous illustrations, the variances can be calculated as follows.

- *Material price variance*:

  actual quantity of material AQ(actual price paid per metre AP – standard price paid per metre SP) = AQ(AP – SP)

  The variance is therefore calculated as 14,000(£6 – £5) = £14,000 adverse.

- *Material usage variance*:

  standard price paid SP(actual quantity of material used AQ – standard quantity of material SQ) = SP(AQ – SQ)

  The variance is therefore calculated as £5(14,000 – 16,000) = £10,000 favourable.

- *Labour rate variance*:

  actual amount of hours AH(actual rate paid per hour AR – standard rate paid per hour SR) = AH(AR – SR)

  The variance is therefore calculated as 20,000(£9 – £8) = £20,000 adverse.

- *Labour efficiency variance*:

  standard rate paid SR(actual amount of hours AH – standard amount of hours SH) = SR(AH – SH)

  The variance is therefore calculated as £8(20,000 – 24,000) = £32,000 favourable.

This illustration shows that the results are the same whichever method is used. In the examination it does not matter which method is used.

Interrelationship between cost variances

Often the cost variances may be inter-linked by a common cause. The reason for one sub-variance can lead to the occurrence of another sub-variance. This is called an interrelationship. In the case study there are two possible interrelationships between the two variances:

- The material is of better quality so the labour force wastes less and therefore appears more efficient.
- The labour is more skilled so the material is not wasted and therefore there is better material usage.

Possible reasons for the cost variances

If we assume that the standard costs are based on reasonable and achievable budgets and are not either ideal standards or basic standards which are out of date, then there are many other reasons which could explain how variances arise. The following is a list of some of the possible causes of variances.

Explanatory notes

- It can therefore be seen that the £12,000 favourable variance is split between the two sub-variances.
- The adverse labour rate variance means that the workforce was paid more per hour than was expected, whereas the favourable efficiency variance shows that the workforce was more efficient than was expected and produced the goods in fewer hours.
- One possible reason for these variances is that the workforce was more skilled and therefore was able to command a higher rate per hour but at the same time was able to be more efficient with its time.
- Of the two variances the adverse rate variance should be investigated to see whether Legin Ltd can employ a cheaper workforce paying less per hour but with the same skills. Labour could be perhaps brought in from overseas which may be cheaper. The large favourable efficiency variance should also be checked as it may be as a result of overestimating the time needed for the production of one unit.

AQA Examiner's tip

In the examination, marks are not just awarded for the calculation of the variance. Always state the variance with both a pound sign and the direction, that is whether the variance is adverse or favourable. There are marks in the examination for the direction and marks could also be lost if a pound sign is not given.

Table 1 *Causes of cost variances*

Variance	Direction	Explanation	Cause
Material price	Adverse	More paid for the material per metre/ kilogram	Higher price charged by supplier
			Unexpected delivery costs
			Better-quality materials
			No bulk discounts
			Scarcity of materials
	Favourable	Less paid for the material per metre/ kilogram	Lower price charged by supplier
			Lower-quality materials
			Unexpected trade/cash discounts
Material usage	Adverse	More materials used for production	Lower-quality material
			Theft, obsolescence, deterioration
			Less-skilled workforce
	Favourable	Fewer materials used for production	Higher, more efficient workforce
			Efficient production processes
			Higher-quality material
Labour rate	Adverse	More paid per hour to the workforce	Unexpected overtime
			Productivity bonuses
			Trade union action
			Rise in minimum wage rates
			Better-skilled workforce
	Favourable	Less paid per hour to the workforce	Lower-grade workforce
			No overtime or bonuses
Labour efficiency	Adverse	More hours used for production	Lower-skilled workforce
			Lower quality of materials
			Unfavourable working conditions
			Lack of training
			Lack of supervision
			Works to rule/strikes (if paid)
			Machine breakdowns
			Lack of materials/orders
			Too many unproductive hours, e.g. coffee breaks
	Favourable	Fewer hours used for production	More-skilled workforce
			Better-quality material
			Fewer non-productive hours
			More training/supervision
			Advances in machine technology

Illustration

How to flex a budget

Flexed approach to variances

The production in month 2 was 4,500 units.

The actual costs for month 2 were as follows.

	£
Direct materials (14,400 metres of material were used)	86,400
Direct labour (20,250 hours of labour were used)	182,250

Fig. 13.19 *Actual costs*

Total material variance

The total material variance was as follows.

	£	
Standard cost (4,500 × £20)	90,000	
Actual cost	86,400	
Total material variance	3,600	favourable

Fig. 13.20 *Total material variance*

Material price

The price per metre is calculated as $\dfrac{£86,400}{14,400} = £6$.

	£	
Standard cost should have been (14,400 × £5)	72,000	
Actual cost (14,400 × £6)	86,400	
Material price variance	14,400	adverse

Fig. 13.21 *Material price variance*

However, as the production levels are different the material usage variance must be flexed.

Therefore the standard expected usage of material for the actual production level is 4 metres per unit × actual production of 4,500 units = 18,000 metres.

Material usage variance

The material usage variance is as follows.

	£	
Standard usage for actual production (4,500 × 4 × £5)	90,000	
Actual usage (14,400 × £5)	72,000	
Material usage variance	18,000	favourable

Fig. 13.22 *Material usage variance*

The calculations of the sub-variances can be checked:

£18,000 favourable – £14,400 adverse = £3,600 favourable total variance

Alternatively, using the formulae

The material price variance is AQ(AP – SP):

14,400(£6 – £5) = £14,400 adverse

The material usage variance is SP(AQ – SQF), where SQF stands for the standard quantity of material flexed for actual production:

£5(14,400 – 18,000) = £18,000 favourable

Total labour variance

The total labour variance was as follows.

	£	
Standard cost (4,500 × £48)	216,000	
Actual cost	182,250	
Total labour variance	33,750	favourable

Fig. 13.23 *Total labour variance*

Labour rate variance

The rate per hour is calculated as $\dfrac{£182,250}{20,250} = £9$.

	£	
Standard cost (20,250 × £8)	162,000	
Actual cost (20,250 × £9)	182,250	
Labour rate variance	20,250	adverse

Fig. 13.24 *Labour rate variance*

However, as the production levels are different again the labour efficiency variance must be flexed.

Therefore the standard expected efficiency of labour at the actual production level is

6 hours per unit × actual production of 4,500 units = 27,000 hours

Labour efficiency variance

The labour efficiency variance is as follows.

	£	
Standard efficiency at actual production (27,000 × £8)	216,000	
Actual efficiency (20,250 × £8)	162,000	
Labour efficiency variance	54,000	favourable

Fig. 13.25 *Labour efficiency variance*

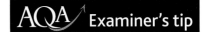

The calculations of sub-variances can be checked:

£54,000 favourable – £20,250 adverse = £33,750 favourable total variance

Alternatively, using the formulae

The labour rate variance is AH(AR – SR):

20,250 (£9 – £8) = £20,250 adverse

The labour efficiency variance is SR(AH – SHF), where SHF stands for standard hours of labour flexed for actual production:

£8(20,250 – 27,000) = £54,000 favourable

The topic of variance analysis is a common examination question that many candidates find difficult. It is recommended that strategies are developed to remember the calculation methods, for example devising a personal mnemonic. However just as important as the calculations are the reasons for these variances, the reconciliations and methods that a business would use to improve results.

Cost reconciliation when production levels are different

In month 2 the amount of production was different to the amount expected. In a cost reconciliation an amendment has to be made to the budgeted cost, namely the budgeted cost for actual production has to be reconciled with the actual cost for actual production.

Cost reconciliation statement for Legin Ltd for month 2

	£ADV	£FAV	£
Budgeted costs (4,500 × £68)			306,000
Material price variance	14,400		
Material usage variance		18,000	
Total variance			(3,600)
Labour rate variance	20,250		
Labour efficiency variance		54,000	
Total variance			(33,750)
Actual cost (86,400 + 182,250)			268,650

Fig. 13.26 *Cost reconciliation statement for month 2*

The reconciliation should reconcile the budgeted costs with the actual costs at the same level of production. In other words it should compare like with like. The only amendment to the cost reconciliation from the procedure used in Fig. 13.12 is to change the budgeted costs for actual production levels.

In this topic you will have learnt:

- how to calculate the total material, labour and revenue (sales) variances and their respective sub-variances
- how to calculate the variances with a flexed budget
- the significance of each variance, including the interrelationships between them
- the meaning of each variance and how businesses use variances
- how to prepare statements reconciling budgeted profit with actual profit and budgeted costs with actual costs.

 Examination-style questions

1 Define the term variance.

2 Explain the terms material price variance and material usage variance.

3 Evaluate the usefulness of calculating variances.

4 Explain why budgets must be flexed when preparing some variances.

5 AQA 2003 Jan ACC7 Q4 (adapted)
The budgeted profit for Handley Enterprises Ltd for the year ended 31 October 2002 is £61,500. The management accountant has calculated the following variances for that year.

	£	
Materials price	2,000	adverse
Materials usage	500	favourable
Labour rate	4,000	favourable
Labour efficiency	1,000	adverse

There are no other variances.

Required
(a) State one possible cause of each of the above variances and explain any possible inter-relationship between them.
(b) Calculate the actual profit for the year ended 31 October 2002.

6   AQA 2005 Jan ACC7 Q1 (adapted)

Dounes Ltd manufactures one product.

The following variances have been calculated for the year ended 31 December 2004.

	£	
Material price	1,400	adverse
Material usage	600	favourable
Labour rate	2,400	favourable
Labour efficiency	900	adverse
Revenue (sales) price	1,800	adverse
Revenue (sales) volume	200	favourable

The budgeted total cost was £124,600.

Calculate the actual total cost for the year ended 31 December 2004.

7   AQA 2008 Jun ACC7 Q2

Spencer Ltd manufactures a single product, the Spenz.

The following information relates to the month of May 2008.

	Budgeted	Actual
Production	2,400 units	2,200 units
Direct material	5 kilos at £5.50 per kilo per unit	£66,000 (13,200 kilos)
Direct labour	6 hours at £4.50 per hour per unit	£70,400 (17,600 hours)

The budgeted profit for May 2008 was £26,000.

Required

(a)   Calculate the material price and material usage sub-variances.

(b)   Calculate the labour rate and labour efficiency sub-variances.

(c)   Calculate the actual profit for Spencer Ltd for the month ended May 2008.

(d)   Explain two possible ways in which the variances will affect the current workforce.

8   AQA 2002 Jun ACC7 Q1

Hall plc manufactures a single product.

The budgeted costs per unit for the month March 2002 were as follows.

	£
Direct materials (£4 per metre)	8.00
Direct labour (£10 per hour)	22.50

The anticipated production for March was 20,000 units.

The actual results for March were as follows.

	£
Materials (40,000 metres)	140,000
Labour (45,000 hours)	405,000

The actual costs were based on the production of 18,500 units.

Required

(a)   Calculate:

i   the material price and usage sub-variances

ii   the labour rate and efficiency sub-variances.

(b)   Explain why these sub-variances may have occurred.

14 Capital investment appraisal

One of the most important decisions which a business will make is whether or not to invest money on a capital item, for example the purchase of a new factory. This expenditure will decrease their liquidity in the short term but must be beneficial in the long term. In this chapter you will learn the techniques used to assess whether an investment of a capital nature should be undertaken from a financial point of view. At the same time in examination questions you would be expected to also consider non-financial consequences of the investment. The topic is called capital investment appraisal.

Topic 1 Payback

In this topic you will learn how to:

- explain what is meant by capital investment and a capital investment appraisal
- explain the concept of payback
- calculate cash inflows, cash outflows and net cash inflows and so make calculations using the payback method of capital investment appraisal
- evaluate the payback method.

Key terms

Capital investment appraisal: the process of using cash flows to decide whether a capital project should be undertaken.

Payback: a calculation of how long it takes to generate enough cash inflows to cover the initial cost of a capital project.

Case study

Jacklyn Ltd

Jacklyn Ltd has manufactured a single product for many years. One of the production machines needs replacing at a cost of £80,000.

What is meant by capital investment appraisal?

Capital investment appraisal is the process of calculating future cash flows of a capital project, for example the purchase of a new machine or capital investment in the development of a new product, in order to make a decision as to whether the capital project should be undertaken.

Two methods of capital investment appraisal are considered within the specification:

- payback
- net present value.

Payback

Payback is the time it takes for the cash inflow generated by a capital project to equal the cash outflow. More simply it is the length of time that is required for the net cash inflows to cover the cost of investment. The shorter the payback period the better. This is especially important if the business has cash-flow problems or will have to borrow the money for the capital project as the inflows can first be used to reduce the loan and then can be used for other potentially income earning purposes.

Illustration

How to calculate payback time

The machine is expected to last 4 years. The financial director of Jacklyn Ltd has calculated the expected cash flows for the new machine as follows.

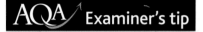

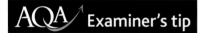

Activity

1 Discuss in pairs the reasons why some businesses need a quick payback period.

	Inflows	Outflows
	£	£
Year 1	50,000	15,000
Year 2	70,000	35,000
Year 3	80,000	40,000
Year 4	90,000	40,000

Fig. 14.1 *Cash flows*

The cash inflows are from the sale of the manufactured goods, whereas the cash outflows are all the production costs, excluding depreciation as this is does not involve the movement of cash.

		Net cash inflows		Cumulative net cash inflows	
		£		£	
Year 1		35,000		35,000	
Year 2	(A)	35,000		70,000	(B)
Year 3		40,000	(C)	110,000	
Year 4		50,000		160,000	

Fig. 14.2 *Cash inflows and outflows*

At the end of year 2 the cumulative net cash inflow was £70,000. Only another £10,000 is needed to cover the cost of the replaced production machine. The payback period is therefore somewhere between the end of year 2 and the end of year 3.

The payback is therefore calculated as:

year with cumulative net cash inflow nearest cost of investment

$$+ \frac{\text{(cost of investment – cumulative net cash inflow nearest year)}}{\text{(net cash inflow of next year)}}$$

$\times$ 365 days/52 weeks/12 months

or

$$A + \frac{\text{(cost of investment – B)}}{C} \times 365 \text{ days/52 weeks/12 months}$$

If the payback for this machine is calculated in years and months, it is therefore

$$2 \text{ years} + \frac{(80,000 - 70,000)}{40,000} \times 12 \text{ months} = 2 \text{ years and 3 months}$$

It therefore takes 2 years and 3 months to make enough net cash inflows to cover the initial cost of the investment of £80,000. Once this period has passed, the business has covered its capital costs.

Note: The answer can also be written in years and days, or years and weeks.

For this illustration, the answer would therefore be 2 years and 91.25 days, or 2 years and 13 weeks.

Advantages and disadvantages of using the payback method of capital investment appraisal

Advantages

- Payback is easy to calculate, understand and is widely used.
- The method is used by many businesses as need for quick cash flow has grown in importance in recent years. It should be remembered that a small manufacturer is unlikely to want to wait long for payback whereas a large organisation can perhaps wait a little longer as it may have better access to cash flow or more reasonable rates of borrowing.

Disadvantages

- Payback ignores the **time value of money**, that is, £3,000 received today does not have the same purchasing value as £3,000 received in three years' time.
- The method ignores the money made after the payback date, for example very little money could be made after the payback date or alternatively considerable money is made after payback. But neither of these possibilities is considered.
- It ignores the whole life of the capital project. The project may last a long time after the payback date during which time large cash inflows are received and/or large outflows are paid out, for example expensive repairs or updating of the capital project. These net cash inflows are ignored, so that a capital project which makes significant net cash inflows over the long term is rejected in favour of a capital project with a quicker payback but which only makes net cash inflows over the short term and quickly needs replacing with another capital project.

> **Key term**
>
> **Time value of money:** this concept states that money received or paid out in the future does not have the same value as money today

In this topic you will have learnt:

- the terms capital investment appraisal and payback
- how to make calculations using the payback method
- how to evaluate the payback method, stating its advantages and disadvantages as a means of capital investment appraisal.

AQA Examination-style questions

1. Explain the term payback.

2. Explain two possible reasons why a business may be interested in a quick payback period.

3. AQA ACC 7 January 2003

   Stanley Standon Ltd is considering the purchase of either machine Elpha or machine Fettan. The following information applies to these machines.

	Elpha	Fettan
	£	£
Purchase price	400,000	500,000
Net cash inflows:		
Year 1	140,000	80,000
Year 2	140,000	120,000
Year 3	140,000	180,000
Year 4	140,000	220,000
Year 5	140,000	280,000

   Both machines are expected to be sold after five years, Elpha for £30,000 and Fettan for £80,000.

   The machine Fettan creates toxic waste. This waste would be disposed of using lorries which would travel through the local town.

   Required
   (a) Calculate the payback period for each machine.
   (b) Which machine would you recommend that Stanley Standon Ltd should purchase? Justify your recommendation.

Topic 2   Net present value

In order to make a meaningful comparison between today's original cost of a capital project and its future net cash inflows, it is necessary to discount the cash inflows back to the present so that they are equivalent in value to a cash inflow now. This enables a like-with-like comparison to be made. The discount factor is called the **cost of capital**, and it is usually based on the weighted average cost of capital available to the business; that is the average cost that is needed to raise the required amount of capital to fund the project.

■ Illustration

How to calculate cost of capital

Jacklyn Ltd has the following capital structure.

		Rate of return	Cost of capital
	£	%	£
Ordinary shares (currently paying a dividend of 12%)	500,000	12	60,000
5% preference shares	200,000	5	10,000
	700,000		70,000

Fig. 14.3 *Capital structure*

The average cost of capital is therefore

$$\frac{\text{cost of capital per annum}}{\text{value of capital}} = \frac{£70,000}{£70,000} = 10\%$$

The **net present value** is therefore the sum of the net cash inflows (future cash inflows less future cash outflows after each has been discounted back to the present) less the initial cost of the investment.

■ If the net present value's answer is positive then the investment could to be undertaken on purely financial grounds. If there is a choice of capital projects then the one with the highest positive net present value should be considered on financial grounds.

■ A negative net present value should be rejected on financial grounds as it means that the sum of future net cash inflows does not cover the initial cost of the investment.

Note: Before a decision can be made whether to undertake an investment all factors need to be considered, that is both financial and non-financial aspects. For example a capital project may yield a high positive net present value but it creates excessive pollution which would create bad publicity for the business adversely affecting revenue (sales), so the decision may be made to invest in the capital project with the lower net present value which does not create excessive pollution.

In this topic you will learn how to:

■ explain the concept of net present value

■ calculate cash inflows, cash outflows and net cash inflows so that net present value can be calculated

■ interpret the results of net present value calculations

■ evaluate the net present value method of capital investment appraisal

■ write a report on a capital investment appraisal using the payback method and the net present value method, including reference to social accounting factors.

Key terms

Cost of capital: the discounting factor used in capital investment appraisals to discount future cash inflows so that they are equivalent in value to cash now.

Net present value: a capital investment appraisal method which uses the present value of net cash inflows to ascertain whether the capital project should be undertaken on financial grounds.

■ Explanatory note

This illustration explains how a business establishes its cost of capital.

■ Illustration

How to calculate net present value

In the case study on Jacklyn Ltd, the net cash inflows were calculated as follows.

	£
Year 1	35,000
Year 2	35,000
Year 3	40,000
Year 4	50,000

Fig. 14.4 *Net cash inflows*

The new machine will cost £80,000.

Additional information:

There is a cost of capital of 10%. This means that it will cost Jacklyn Ltd £8,000 (10% of the £80,000) to raise the capital to fund the new machine.

The discount factors are as follows.

	Discount factor
Year 1	0.909
Year 2	0.826
Year 3	0.751
Year 4	0.683

Fig. 14.5 *Discount factors*

AQA Examiner's tip

In the examination, the discount factors will be given at a specified cost of capital. You are not expected to calculate them.

Year	Net cash inflow	×	Discount factor	=	Present value
	£				£
0	(80,000)		1.000		(80,000)
1	35,000		0.909		31,815
2	35,000		0.826		28,910
3	40,000		0.751		30,040
4	50,000		0.683		34,150
	80,000			Net present value:	44,915

Fig. 14.6 *Statement to calculate net present value of machine*

Explanatory notes

- In year 0, the discount factor is 1 as there has been no passage of time so there is no change in the value of money.
- In year 1, the discount factor is 0.909 as a year has passed. The net cash inflow of £35,000 is multiplied by 0.909 to give a present value of £31,815.
- This process continues throughout the life of the machine with the discount factor reducing as time passes.
- At the end of the life of the machine, the total of net cash inflows of £80,000 has a total positive net present value of £44,915. The positive net present value means that from a financial point of view, the machine should be purchased, as the discounted present value of the net cash inflows exceeds the initial cost of the machine. (The minimum acceptable solution is a zero net present value, as this means that there is a balance with the cost of funds.)

Advantages and disadvantages of using net present value as a method of capital investment appraisal

Advantages

- This method considers the time value of money by using the discount factors.
- It includes all the net cash inflows from the whole life of the capital project.

Disadvantages

- It is more complex to calculate than the payback method.
- It is based around selecting the relevant cost of capital which may be difficult to determine with any reliability. The higher the cost of capital, the lower the net present value.
- It should not be considered on its own, for the project may still not be worth investing in due to the social non-financial factors and a slow payback which could outweigh the benefit of the positive net present value.

Writing a report on a potential capital investment

Often a requirement in the examination is to write a report on a potential capital investment project assessing whether the business should invest in the project or not. When evaluating a capital investment project it is expected that the candidate will give a balanced answer of both the benefits and limitations of investing in the project considering both financial and non-financial factors.

Illustration

How to write a report on a potential capital investment project

Additional information:

Jacklyn Ltd will have to borrow the money to pay for the new machine. This debt has to be paid back over 3 years. It is also expected that the workforce will have to be trained how to use the new machine. The carbon footprint is expected to be higher with this machine.

Report contents should include, among other factors, the following.

Link

Link to Chapter 16, Social accounting of this book.

AQA Examiner's tip

In all reports there should be an evaluative process, with a balanced view whereby both sides of the argument are given and a final recommendation is made with a summarised justification. There will be several marks in the examination for these judgements.

Financial considerations:

- The payback is in a short period of time and before the debt has to repaid back to the bank.
- The training of the workforce will cost time and money.
- There will be finance costs (interest) to pay on the debt. Was this included in the outflows? If not it is an extra cost which needs to be considered.
- Borrowing for this machine may reduce the opportunities of borrowing to fund other areas of the business, for example health and safety.
- How long is the machine expected to last or will it need replacing not long after the payback period?
- Can the machine be leased and not purchased. This may be a cheaper option which will mean that there is no need to borrow from the bank which will aid cash flow and stop finance costs (interest) being paid, which is dead money.
- The net present value is positive at a cost of capital of 10%.

Non-financial considerations:

- Some of the workforce may feel threatened by the introduction of a new machine and may resist change by not wanting to be retrained.
- Staff may fear being replaced by the machine and may be demotivated by the lack of money put into other areas of the business.
- Staff may be concerned at the lack of liquidity within the business and may be concerned that there will be no future wage rises or productivity bonuses. This will cause a fall in morale.
- How much disruption will there be whilst the machine is being replaced?
- Can the production process continue without the machine being replaced? If not then unless there are cheaper alternative replacement machines, then this machine must be purchased.
- Will the increase in carbon footprint result in action by outside pressure groups including government agencies which may distrupt production?

Final recommendation:

The machine appears to have a relatively quick payback and a positive net present value, so if the machine lasts for at least several more years, and if staff can overcome their concerns, then it is recommended that the business purchase the machine.

In this topic you will have learnt:

- the term net present value
- how to calculate the expected net cash inflows from a capital project and from these calculate the net present value
- how to interpret the resulting net present value in that, if it is positive, the project should be undertaken from a financial point of view, and if it is negative it should be rejected
- how to evaluate the net present value, stating its advantages and disadvantages as a method of capital investment appraisal
- how to write a report on a capital investment appraisal using net present value and payback, including reference to social accounting.

1   Explain the terms net present value, payback and cost of capital.

2   Identify the advantages and disadvantages of using
        (a)   the payback method of capital investment appraisal
        (b)   the net present value methods of capital investment appraisal.

3   AQA 2002 Jun ACC7 Q (amended)

        The main cutting machine of MV Wilkins Ltd needs to be replaced. A replacement machine will cost £300,000.

        The current machine cuts 40,000 units a year. The number of units cut is expected to be reduced by 10% in year 1 due to the time taken to install the new machine. The number of units cut is expected to increase to 42,000 units for year 2 and year 3 respectively.

        Additional information:

        ▓   The cost of capital is 10%.

        ▓   The following is an extract from the present value table for £1.

	10%
Year 1	0.909
Year 2	0.826
Year 3	0.751

        ▓   It is assumed that revenues are received and costs are paid at the end of the year.
        ▓   Each unit of production costs £12 to manufacture.
        ▓   Each unit is expected to sell for £15 in years 1 and 2, increasing by 5% in year 3.
        ▓   It is assumed that everything produced is sold.

        Required

        (a)   Calculate the annual net cash flows for each year, which are expected to result from the purchase of the machine.

        (b)   Using the expected annual net cash flows, calculate the net present value for the replacement machine.

        (c)   State whether or not MV Wilkins Ltd should purchase the machine. Give one reason for your answer.

4   AQA 2008 Jun ACC7 Q1 a–d

        One of the assembly machines at Roberts Ltd needs to be replaced.

        A replacement machine will cost £200,000, which is payable on purchase.

        The replacement machine is expected to last 4 years, but will need a complete maintenance check in year 3 at a cost of £50,000.

        The existing machine assembles 4,000 units a year. The number of units assembled by the replacement machine is expected to be 25% lower in year 1 than the existing machine due to the time lost during installation and testing. In year 2 it is expected that 4,500 units will be assembled and this will increase by 20% each year compared to the previous year.

        The existing machine produces units at a cost of £26 each, whereas the replacement machine will produce units at a cost of £24 each. The selling price is currently £42 per unit but with the improved quality provided by the replacement machine this will increase to £45 per unit. From year 3, it is expected that the cost of manufacture will increase by 25% each year and the selling price will increase by 30% each year compared to the previous year.

The cost of capital is 14%.

The following is an extract from the present value table for £1.

	14%
Year 1	0.877
Year 2	0.769
Year 3	0.675
Year 4	0.592

It is assumed that all units produced are sold.

Required

(a)   Calculate the expected net cash flows for each year, using the replacement machine.

(b)   Calculate the payback period for the replacement machine.

(c)   Calculate the net present value for the replacement machine using the expected net cash flows. Assume that revenues are received and costs are paid at the end of each year.

(d)   Compare the two methods of capital investment appraisal.

5   AQA 2005 Jan ACC7 Q3

Wesley Rise wishes to purchase a machine with an initial cost of £180,000 plus a delivery charge of £20,000. The machine is expected to last 5 years.

The cost of capital is 12%. The discount factors at this cost of capital are as follows.

	Discount factor
Year 1	0.893
Year 2	0.797
Year 3	0.712
Year 4	0.636
Year 5	0.567

The cash inflows generated by the machine are expected to be as shown below.

	£
Year 1	60,000
Year 2	80,000
Year 3	120,000
Year 4	120,000
Year 5	80,000

The cash outflows are expected to be £40,000 each year. A major overhaul of the machine is expected to be carried out at a cost of £20,000 in year 4.

Required

(a)   Calculate the payback period for the machine.

(b)   Calculate the net present value for the machine.

(c)   Advise whether the machine should be purchased. Give reasons for your decision.

15 Budgeting

At AS level you were introduced to the principles of budgeting through the use of the cash budget (as described in chapter 10 of the AS textbook). You will already understand that a cash budget can give information to the owners and managers of a business so they can make more informed decisions, for example how much money they are expected to have in the bank in three months' time, as well as the expected sources of the money coming into the business and the levels of expenditure. But the cash budget is not the only budget used by a business. There are many others. In this chapter you will learn some of the other types of budget, as well as the benefits and limitations of budgetary control.

Topic 1   Budgetary control

In this chapter you will learn how to:

- explain the benefits of budgetary control

- explain the limitations of budgetary control

- evaluate budgetary control.

Key terms

Budget: a financial plan for the future expressed in quantitative terms. It is used to control the use of resources so that the business objectives can be achieved.

Master budget: taken from the functional budgets and consists of a budgeted profit and loss account and forecast balance sheet.

Budgeting: the preparation of the budgets.

Budget centre: a department or area for which a budget has been set up.

Budgetary control: responsibility to achieve the budget has been delegated to the budget centre managers.

What is budgetary control?

A **budget** is a short-term financial plan of standard costs and revenues prepared for the future to control resources so that the business objectives can be achieved. All functional budgets are used to prepare the **master budget**, which is a budgeted profit and loss account and forecast balance sheet. **Budgeting** is the preparation of the budgets for each **budget centre**, and **budgetary control** is when each budget centre manager has responsibility to:

- justifiably use resources

- control costs

- achieve the activities set by the budget in accordance with the business's objectives.

Each manager's performance is then evaluated by comparing actual results against the targets set for the budget centre, so any underachievement can be analysed and any remedial action can be taken.

Benefits of budgeting

The benefits of budgeting fall into the following main categories.

- Control: A budget is a formal authorisation to a budget centre manager of a specified amount to be allocated to specified activities, thereby resources such as cash and labour hours are controlled.

- Planning: By using a budget, the use of resources, for example cash, materials and labour hours, is planned in order to achieve the objectives of the business.

- Communication and coordination: Budgets communicate plans to managers responsible for carrying them out. They also ensure coordination between managers of sub-units so that each is aware of the others' requirements, for example between the stores, production and sales departments.

Link

See *AQA AS Accounting*, Unit 2, where budgeting is introduced.

- Motivation: Budgets are often intended to motivate managers to perform in line with organisational objectives. This especially applies if the managers had been included in the drawing up of the budgets, which will then be realistic and achievable, and if there are rewards for achievement of the budget targets.

- Performance evaluation and monitoring: The performance of managers is often evaluated by reference to budgetary standards. Any variance between the budget and actual results will then be assessed and corrective action taken.

- Aid to decision-making: If each manager bases their decision-making around their budget then all departmental decisions will relate to the corporate plan and business objectives.

Limitations of budgetary control

The limitations of using budgetary control are as follows.

- A budget must be produced within the limiting factors that surround the business, for example the amount of market demand for its product; the number of skilled employees available; the availability of material supplies; the space available either as a working area or for storage; the amount of cash or credit facilities available to finance the business.

- A budget which is unrealistic or unachievable is of limited use and may do more harm than good, especially considering the negative effect it will have on the workforce who will feel that they are underperforming and their productivity may decline further.

- Likewise a budget must not be set too low as this is also demotivational. This can happen when there is no goal congruence, or agreement, between the objectives of the manager and the objectives of the business. A manager may feel that the budget is to be used to evaluate and judge his performance and so may endeavour to set the budget to an easily achievable target, which at the same time may not motivate his team.

- Budgets can restrict activity so that managers are not innovative and fail to take advantage of unexpected opportunities as their actions are too strictly controlled.

- Through careful control of their budgets throughout the year managers may have a surplus available at the end of the year, but rather than save this surplus they will spend it so their budget will not be reduced next year. So budgets may inadvertently encourage the waste or inefficient use of resources.

In summary, a budget is only as useful as the standards used to set it. If set too high it is unachievable and demotivates the workforce, and if set too low it fails to motivate and can lead to inefficiencies and an unproductive workforce.

AQA Examiner's tip

In examinations, benefits and limitations must be applied to the scenario of the question with careful note taken as to whether the business provides a service or produces a product.

In this topic you will have learnt:

- the benefits of budgetary control

- the limitations of budgetary control

- how to evaluate budgetary control.

1   Explain the term budgetary control.

2   Explain how the many ways in which setting a budget can be constricted.

3   'Departmental managers should be left to their own devices as then they are free to act in an unrestricted manner and so innovation will be achieved.' Discuss.

Topic 2   Preparing and commenting on budgets

In this chapter you will learn how to:

- prepare a range of budgets

- prepare a set of forecast final accounts

- evaluate the performance of a business based on budgeted information

- make recommendations as to how the performance of a business, as revealed by a budget, could be improved.

 Examiner's tip

All budgets usually have a vertical breakdown of data for each period or month.

Key term

Revenue (sales) budget: a summary of the expected revenue (sales) units and revenue (sales) value for the future.

Case study

Nawor Halls

Nawor Halls owns a business which manufactures a single product, the Conny. The business operates over 13 periods a year. Each period consists of four weeks with five working days in each week. Last year Nawor had a fixed production of 6,000 units per period regardless of the level of revenue (sales), but this year he wants to introduce a system of budgetary control.

Types of budget

The following are types of functional budget:

- **revenue (sales) budget**
- production budget
- purchases budget
- labour budget
- trade receivables (trade debtors) budget
- trade payables (trade creditors) budget
- cash budget (already covered in *AQA AS Accounting*, Unit 2).

Revenue (sales) budget

The revenue (sales) budget records the amount of units expected to be sold as well as the expected revenue (sales) value per period.

■ Illustration

How to prepare a sales budget

The following information is available for Nawor Halls for the first four periods of the new year.

	Period 1	Period 2	Period 3	Period 4
Expected revenue (sales) (units)	1,200	1,400	1,500	1,400

Fig. 15.1 *Cash flows*

Each unit of Conny sells for £100.

Revenue (sales) budget of Nawor Halls

	Period 1	Period 2	Period 3	Period 4
Revenue (sales) units	1,200	1,400	1,500	1,400
Revenue (sales) value (units × price)	£120,000	£140,000	£150,000	£140,000

Fig. 15.2 *Revenue (sales) budget for Nawor Halls*

This is a forecast predicting what the revenue (sales) will be in the future, perhaps based on previous periods' revenue (sales) or from market research.

Production budget

The **production budget** is the key budget as all production costs will be based on the quantities stated within this budget.

■ Illustration

How to prepare a production budget

Nawor Halls maintains closing inventory (stock) at a level sufficient to cover 8 days of revenue (sales) for the next period. However, storage constraints restrict inventory (stock) to a maximum of 580 units. It is assumed that revenue (sales) accrues evenly within each period. At the start of period 1 there are expected to be 480 units in inventory (stock).

Production budget of Nawor Halls

	Period 1	Period 2	Period 3
	Units	Units	Units
Revenue (sales)	1,200	1,400	1,500
Opening inventory (stock)	(480)	(560)	(580)
Closing inventory (stock) (restricted)	560	580	560
Production	1,280	1,420	1,480

Fig. 15.3 *Production budget for Nawor Halls for the first three periods*

- This budget is in units only and is coordinated with the information from the revenue (sales) budget.

- The closing inventory (stock) is equivalent to 8 days of next period's revenue (sales). There are 20 days in a period (13 periods a year, each period has 4 weeks with 5 days in a week). Closing inventory (stock) is therefore calculated as $8/20 \times$ next period's revenue (sales), for example for period 1 closing inventory (stock) is calculated as $8/20 \times 1,400 = 560$. Due to storage restrictions the amount in closing inventory (stock) is limited to a maximum of 580 units. The business can therefore be seen in period 2 to be working to maximum capacity.

- The closing inventory (stock) of one month becomes the opening inventory (stock) of the next month.

- The units of production are calculated as revenue (sales) – opening inventory (stock) + closing inventory (stock) units.

Purchases budget

The **purchases budget** provides information on the cost of materials.

How to prepare a purchases budget

Each Conny consists of 2 metres of material, which costs £15 per metre. The material cost per unit is therefore £30.

Purchases budget for Nawor Halls

	Period 1	Period 2	Period 3
Production units	1,280	1,420	1,480
Material cost (£15 × units)	£38,400	£42,600	£44,400

Fig. 15.4 *Purchases budget for Nawor Halls for the first three periods*

Nawor Halls can therefore see from this budget that the cost of purchases is increasing in line with the level of production. Perhaps he should negotiate a bulk-buying discount with the suppliers.

Labour budget

The **labour budget** is new to the specification. It identifies the amount of labour hours required to produce the levels of production stated in the production budget. The labour budget also helps management plan work patterns, for example shifts, as well as calculating the expected labour costs.

How to prepare a labour budget

Each Conny takes 2 hours in the machining department and 3 hours in the assembly department.

The workforce is paid £96 for each shift in the machining department and £60 for each shift in the assembly department.

Machinists complete an 8 hour shift and workers in the assembly department complete a 6 hour shift.

Labour budget for Nawor Halls

		Period 1	Period 2	Period 3
Units produced		1,280	1,420	1,480
Machining department:				
Machining hours (× 2)		2,560 hours	2,840 hours	2,960 hours
Number of 8 hour shifts		320	355	370
Labour cost (machining department)	A	£30,720	£34,080	£35,520
Assembly department:				
Assembly hours (× 3)		3,840 hours	4,260 hours	4,440 hours
Number of 6 hour shifts		640	710	740
Labour cost (assembly department)	B	£38,400	£42,600	£44,400
Total labour cost	A + B	£69,120	£76,680	£79,920

Fig. 15.5 *Labour budget for Nawor Halls for the first three periods*

Explanatory notes

- The budget is coordinated with information from the production budget.
- Machining department:
  - a Each unit spends 2 hours in the machining department so multiply the number of units produced by 2 to calculate the total number of hours.
  - b Each shift takes 8 hours so divide the total number of hours by 8 to achieve the number of shifts.
  - c Each shift costs £96 in the machining department so multiply the number of shifts by 96 to achieve the total labour cost for the machining department.(A)
- Assembly department:
  - a Each unit spends 3 hours in the assembly department so multiply the number of units produced by 3 to calculate the total number of hours.
  - b Each shift takes 6 hours so divide the total number of hours by 6 to achieve the number of shifts.
  - c Each shift costs £60 in the assembly department so multiply the number of shifts by 60 to achieve the total labour cost for the assembly department.(B)
- Total labour cost for each period: This is calculated by adding A and B together for each period.
- The labour budget illustrates that if every worker works 5 shifts a week the maximum number of machinists he needs is in period 3 (370/5 = 74) and the maximum number of assembly workers is also needed in period 3 (740/5 = 148).

Trade receivables (trade debtors) budget

The **trade receivables (trade debtors) budget** identifies the amount of money expected to be owed by customers each period.

Illustration

How to prepare a trade receivables (debtors) budget

Nawor Halls expects 20% of each period's revenue (sales) to be paid in cash. Therefore 80% of each period's revenue (sales) will be on credit terms – half of the credit revenue (sales) will pay after one period and the other half will pay after two periods. At the start of period 1 there are trade receivables (trade debtors) of £80,000 of which half will pay during the first period and the other half will pay in the second period. There was also a debt from two periods before of £45,000 which is expected to be paid in period 1. £10,000 of this debt is expected to be a bad debt.

Trade receivables (trade debtors) budget for Nawor Halls

	Period 1	Period 2	Period 3
	£	£	£
Balance b/f	80,000	81,000	105,000
Credit revenue (sales)	96,000	112,000	120,000
Receipts (credit revenue (sales) from previous period)	(40,000)	(48,000)	(56,000)
Receipts (credit revenue (sales) from two periods before)	(35,000)	(40,000)	(48,000)
Bad debt	(10,000)	–	–
Balance c/f	81,000	105,000	121,000

Fig. 15.6 *Trade receivables (trade debtors) budget for Nawor Halls for the first three periods*

Explanatory notes

■ This budget is coordinated with the revenue (sales) budget.

■ Credit revenue (sales): These are calculated as total revenue (sales) less 20% (cash receipts). For example in period 1 the total revenue (sales) are £120,000 less the cash receipts of £24,000 = £96,000 credit revenue (sales).

■ Receipts:

  a Half of the credit revenue (sales) are received after one month and the other half two months later. For example in period 1 the credit revenue (sales) are £96,000 of which half will pay in period 2 and the other half in period 3.

  b In period 1 the receipts from credit revenue (sales) are from trade receivables (debtors) from the previous year, who are one period old and therefore half (£40,000) will be received in period 1 and the other half in period 2.

  c In period 1 there are also receipts from credit revenue (sales) which are from receivables (debtors) from the previous year who are two periods old and therefore all will be received in period 1. However an adjustment must be made for £10,000 of this debt which is bad and will not be recovered. The bad debt is recorded separately.

■ Balance c/f: The balance c/f is the amount of trade receivables (trade debtors) outstanding for the period and is carried forward to the next period and recorded as balance brought forward.

■ It can clearly be seen that that the amount of trade receivables (trade debtors) is increasing therefore so is the risk of further bad debts. Nawor Halls should try to encourage more cash revenue (sales) perhaps by increasing the amount of cash discount.

Trade payables (trade creditors) budget

The **trade payables (trade creditors) budget** identifies the amount of money owed to suppliers at the end of each period.

Illustration

How to prepare a trade payables (trade creditors) budget

Nawor Halls pays for 25% of his purchases by cash. Therefore 75% of each period's purchases are on credit terms. 80% of the credit purchases are paid after one period and 20% will pay after two periods. At the start of period 1 there are £22,500 of trade payables (creditors) of which £18,000 will be paid in the first period and the rest will be paid in the second period. There is also an amount owing from two periods before of £4,000 which is expected to be paid in period 1.

Trade payable (trade creditors) budget for Nawor Halls

	Period 1	Period 2	Period 3
	£	£	£
Balance b/f	22,500	29,300	33,710
Credit purchases	28,800	31,950	33,300
Payments (credit purchases from previous period)	(18,000)	(23,040)	(25,560)
Payments (credit purchases from two periods before)	(4,000)	(4,500)	(5,760)
Balance c/f	29,300	33,710	35,690

Fig. 15.7 Trade payables (trade creditors) budget for Nawor Halls for the first three periods

Explanatory notes

- This budget is coordinated with the purchases budget.
- Credit purchases: These are calculated as total purchase less 25% (cash payments) For example in period 1 the total purchases are £38,400 less the cash payments of £9,600 = £28,800 credit purchases.
- Payments:
  - a 80% of the credit purchases are paid after one month and 20% two months later. For example in period 1 the credit purchases are £28,800, of which 80% (£23,040) will be paid in period 2 and the 20% (£5,760) in period 3.
  - b In period 1, the payments to credit purchases are to trade payables (creditors) from the previous year, who are one period old, and therefore 80% (£18,000) will be paid in period 1 and 20% (£4,500) in period 2.
  - c In period 1, there are also payments to credit purchases which are to trade payables (trade creditors) from the previous year who are two periods old and therefore all will be paid in period 1.
- Balance c/f: The balance carried forward is the amount of trade payables (creditors) outstanding for the period and is carried forward to the next period and recorded as the balance brought forward.
- It can clearly be seen that Nawor Halls owes an increasing amount to his trade payables (trade creditors).

Master budget

Information is taken from all of the functional budgets and a set of forecast financial statements is produced. This is known as the master budget.

Illustration

How to prepare the master budget

Nawor Halls wishes to produce a set of forecast financial statements from his functional budgets as a means of evaluating his expected profitability.

Notes:

- The standard cost per unit is as follows.

	£
Direct materials	30
Direct labour (24 + 30)	54
	84

Fig. 15.8 *Standard cost per unit*

- Inventory (stock) will be valued on the basis of the standard cost per unit.
- Overheads for the period are expected to be £45,600
- It is assumed that there is no opening or closing inventory (stock) of raw materials or work in progress.

	£	£
Revenue (sales) (1,200 + 1,400 + 1,500 units) × £100		410,000
Opening inventory (stock) (480 units × £84)	40,320	
Cost of production (1,280 + 1,420 + 1,480) × £84*	351,120	
Closing inventory (stock) (560 units × £84)	(47,040)	
Cost of sales (cost of goods sold)		(344,400)
Gross profit		65,600
Bad debt	10,000	
Overheads	45,600	
		(55,600)
Profit for the year		10,000

Fig. 15.9 *Forecast income statement (trading account) for Nawor Halls for the first three periods*

Additional information:

- The fixed assets were expected to have a book value of £142,000.
- The balance at the bank was expected to be £15,300.
- The amount owing on a long-term loan was expected to be £10,000.
- The capital brought forward was expected to be £326,310.
- The drawings for the period were expected to be £5,660.

Explanatory notes

- Closing inventory (stock) is the amount in the income statement which is calculated by multiplying the closing inventory (stock) in period 3 from the production budget by the standard cost.

- Trade receivables (trade debtors) is calculated using the trade receivables (trade debtors) budgets as the trade receivables (trade debtors) from period 2 (half of period 2's credit revenue (sales), £56,000) plus the trade receivables (trade debtors) from period 3 (all of period 3's credit revenue (sales), £120,000).

- Trade payables (trade creditors) is calculated using the trade payables (trade creditors) budget as the trade payables (trade creditors) from period 2 (20% of period 2's credit purchases, £6,390) plus the trade payables (trade creditors) from period 3 (all of period 3's credit purchases, £33,300).

	£	£
Non-current (fixed) assets		142,000
Current assets:		
Inventory (stock)	47,040	
Trade receivables (trade debtors)	176,000	
Bank	15,300	
	238,340	
Current liabilities:		
Trade payables (trade creditors)	(39,690)	
Working capital		198,650
		340,650
Non-current (long-term) liabilities:		
Long-term loan		(10,000)
		330,650
Financed by:		
Capital b/f		326,310
Profit for the year		10,000
Drawings		(5,660)
		330,650

Fig. 15.10 *Forecast balance sheet for Nawor Halls at the end of period 3*

Nawor Halls can see from the forecast financial statements that he does expect to make a profit, albeit a small one. He is expected to have both a positive working capital and money in the bank (which would be ascertained from a cash budget). He must ensure that he does not increase the level of his drawings too much. He has a considerable amount of trade receivables (trade debtors) which needs careful monitoring otherwise he opens himself up to the possibility of bad debts. So it is recommended that he looks into reducing the level of trade receivables (trade debtors).

In this topic you will have learnt:

- how to prepare a range of budgets
- how to prepare a set of forecast financial statements (final accounts)
- how to evaluate the performance of a business on the basis of budgeted information
- how to make recommendations as to how the performance of a business, as revealed by a budget, could be improved.

1 Explain the term budget.

2 Identify a budget which is not useful to the following businesses:

- a school
- a firm of accountants
- a leisure complex
- a high street butcher.

Give a reason why the budget is not useful.

3 Identify two uses for each of the following budgets:

- a labour budget
- a production budget
- a trade receivables (trade debtors) budget.

4 AQA 2007 Jun ACC4 Q3 a

Damir Ltd is a small business which manufactures toys.

The following information is available for the next four months.

	January	February	March	April
Expected revenue (sales) (units)	2,000	2,200	2,300	2,200

Additional information:

(a) Each unit sells for £15.

(b) Each month, 20% of revenue (sales) is expected to be on a cash basis.

(c) Fifty per cent of trade receivables (trade debtors) are expected to pay after one month. The remainder are expected to pay after two months.

(d) Trade receivables (trade debtors) on 1 January are expected to be:

- £21,600 from December revenue (sales), of which £10,800 will be paid in January and the balance in February
- £7,200 from November revenue (sales), which will be paid in January.

Required

Prepare a receivables (trade debtors) budget for Damir Ltd for *each* of the four months January to April.

5 AQA 2008 Jun ACC7 Q3

Jameson Ltd operates over 13 periods a year. Each period consists of four weeks with five working days in each week.

The revenue (sales) for the next four periods are expected to be as follows.

	Period 1	Period 2	Period 3	Period 4
Units	11,500	12,000	14,000	12,500

Assume that sales accrue evenly within each period.

The inventory (stock) at the start of period 1 was 4,600 units. It is the policy to maintain the closing inventory (stock) of units at a level which is sufficient to cover 8 days of revenue (sales) for the next period. However, storage constraints restrict inventory (stock) to a maximum of 5,000 units.

Prepare the production budget in units for each period for periods 1–3.

6   AQA 2008 Jun ACC4 Q2

Svetlana Omarova owns a business manufacturing drinking mugs.

The business operates over 13 four-week periods with five working days in each week.

Previously, Svetlana had fixed production at 18,000 mugs per period, regardless of the level of revenue (sales). This year Svetlana has decided to introduce a system of budgetary control.

The revenue (sales) for the first four periods of this year are expected to be as follows:

	Period 1	Period 2	Period 3	Period 4
Mugs (units)	14,500	15,200	16,100	1, 400

Revenues (sales) are expected to occur evenly throughout each period.

Each mug costs 60p to make and is sold for £1.45.

Inventory (stock) at the start of period 1 is 2,900 mugs. Inventory (stock) is now to be maintained at a level sufficient to cover four days of the next period's expected revenue (sales).

Required

(a)   Prepare the production budget in units for each of the periods 1–3.

(b)   Explain two benefits for Svetlana's business of introducing a system of budgetary control.

7   Vassilya owns a business manufacturing a single product.

Her production for the first four months is expected to be as follows.

	Month 1	Month 2	Month 3	Month 4
Production in units	800	1,050	1,350	1,650

Each unit takes 2.5 hours to manufacture. The workers are paid £8 per hour when working a 40-hour week and £11 per hour when working overtime. There are 75 workers.

Vassilya is pleased with the increase in production which has resulted from an expected increase in revenue (sales), but is concerned with the extra labour costs arising through overtime being paid.

(a)   Prepare a labour budget to calculate the number of hours needed to fulfil expected production and the cost of labour, including the cost of overtime.

Vassilya does not want any spare capacity and wants her workers to work a fully productive month so that inventory (stock) can be produced in advance in preparation for the increased revenue (sales) in months 3 and 4.

(b)   Prepare a labour budget avoiding overtime. Identify the production in units, the hours and workers needed. Identify any shortfall in production where overtime will have to be paid to satisfy demand.

16 Social accounting

In this chapter you will learn how to:

- explain the term social accounting

- demonstrate an awareness of non-financial factors to be considered in decision making

- make critical assessments of decisions from ethical and non-financial standpoints.

So far in the A level course you have learnt about both financial accounting, for example the drawing up of the final accounts and balance sheet of different business structures, and management and cost accounting, for example the various budgets within budgetary control. Both of these include financial calculations. But accounting decisions are not based on financial implications alone as non-financial implications need to be considered as well before a decision can be made. This chapter deals with those non-financial considerations.

Case study

Mihail Danov

Mihail Danov is considering buying an outlet in a rural area. Previously the outlet was used as a farm store. Mihail intends to expand the building into a plastics factory which will enable him to increase his output by 20% and thereby increase profits in the long term once the costs of set-up have been covered. The new factory will include a large chimney which will expel pollution into the air. He will have to apply to the local council for permission to expand but believes he will be successful as the new factory will bring employment to the local area.

Key terms

Social accounting: this term is applied when businesses are accountable to society at large, whereby they must consider both the non-financial and financial aspects of every decision they make.

Stakeholders: any group or individual who has an interest in the activities of the business.

Social accounting

Social accounting is the term used to describe social accountability, whereby businesses must consider the non-financial as well as the financial aspects of any decisions which they make. It is argued that businesses must not be driven by the motive of profit maximisation alone, but must also consider the wider aspects of each decision. Consideration must be given as to how internal decisions can also affect external **stakeholders**, such as the local community, the workforce, the environment and society at large. Social accounting recognises that any business which fails to consider the accountability to society of its decisions may find that some of those decisions are counter-productive and that profitability falls as society responds negatively to their actions. One example would be the bad publicity given by the media to some of the petrol companies, accusing them of causing environmental damage to the sea and sea life by having defective and leaking pipes, which resulted in Greenpeace action and boycotting of the companies' petrol garages on publicised days. Similarly, an unhappy workforce may cause a fall in productivity if they perceive that the company is trying to save money by failing to maintain health and safety standards.

AQA Examiner's tip

Sometimes it is difficult to ascertain which factors are financial and which are non-financial as it is often believed that all the decisions that a business makes are in the end financial as they will affect profitability. In general though the examiner considers that if figures are given in the question, any use of these figures will give a financial argument and any ethical assessment is non-financial.

How to write a report that includes non-financial considerations

Write a report to Mihail explaining the financial and non-financial considerations of his decision to expand the rural outlet.

To: Mihail

From: Student

Date: Date of examination

Subject: An analysis of the implications of expanding the rural outlet

This report could include the following.

Financial considerations

- What is the cost of the expansion?
- How long will it take to complete the expansion?
- Will the market be able to sustain the increase in output? Will competitors react by decreasing their prices and entering a price war?
- How long will the business have to wait until profits are made? Does the business have to borrow the money to pay for the expansion? If so, what is the interest rate?
- What financial backing is needed for the finance? Will Mihail have to put up his own possessions as security for the loan?
- Will there be any costs to consider if legal action is taken against the business because of the pollution?

Non-financial considerations

- Will Mihail have to pay for a change of purpose for the farm store to be expanded into a factory? If so, how long will this take and can it be guaranteed?
- Will the local infrastructure be adequate for the increase in transport etc.?
- Are there transport links for the workforce to be able to travel to work? If not, are there a sufficient number of people for the workforce in the local area? Does the local community have enough skilled workers?
- What damage can pressure groups, for example environmentalists, do to the reputation of the business? Will they be able to stop or hinder the activities of the business in any way, for example by picketing outside the factory?
- Are there any legal implications of knowingly polluting the air?
- Will there be restrictions on the activities, for example only using the chimney between certain hours?
- How is the local community expected to react? Will there be petitions against the chimney and bad press?

Explanatory note

The report does not include any benefits of the expansion to the local community as the question only asks for considerations from Mihail's point of view. These could only be included if they resulted in good publicity for Mihail.

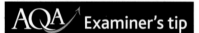

AQA Examiner's tip

A question on social accounting is to be expected in the examination paper. Although not guaranteed, often a question requires a report or prose answer to a scenario considering both the financial and non-financial aspects from the point of view of a particular stakeholder. Remember that although there is not a definite right or wrong answer, the examiner is looking for an evaluative answer which looks at both sides of the argument and comes to a final judgement.

Recommendation:

It appears that there could be considerable costs associated with expansion. It is recommended that investigations are made into whether a factory site can be found in a more urban area or whether an alternative production method can be used that does not necessitate the use of a chimney that causes pollution. It is recommended that Mihail does not buy the outlet until more consideration has been given to alternatives.

Examples of possible social accounting scenarios

Table 1 *Social accounting scenarios*

Scenario	Stakeholders affected	Possible considerations
New machine or plant which causes pollution	Employees	Ill health, refusal to work, strike action
	Local community	Drop in house prices, residents moving away, decline in area
	Environmental pressure groups	Bad publicity, picketing, boycotting product
	Owners (shareholders)	Bad publicity reducing share prices
Replacement of staff through redundancy by robotics	Employees	Loss of jobs, remaining employees demotivated as fearful of losing their own jobs, low morale
	Banks/lenders	Concerns over cost of redundancies, security of loans
	Owners	Bad publicity in short term but hope of future profits
	Local community	Local unemployment, decline in area as workers move away to search for employment
	Trade unions	May take action to prevent job losses
Introduction of cheaper harmful product to product range	Customers	May refuse to buy and look to competitors
	Workforce	May refuse to work because of health concerns
	Suppliers	May have reputation harmed by association
	Owners (shareholders)	Bad publicity may reduce share price
	Trade unions	May take action on employees' behalf
	Pressure groups	Bad publicity, picketing, boycotting product
	Competitors	May underprice to increase market share

These are only some examples from a very wide range of possible scenarios.

AQA Examiner's tip

Always ensure that answers are from the perspective asked for in the question. For example, if the question asks the student to evaluate a business decision from the workforce's point of view, then there are no marks for answering from the owners'. This will achieve no marks, however valid the comments. This also applies to general comments!

Activity

1 Work in a group of four. Decide on a topical business proposal. One group is to think of the financial arguments for going ahead with the proposal. The other group is to think of the non-financial factors against the decision. Both groups are to present their arguments to the rest of the class. The class is to make a final decision as to whether the proposal is to go ahead. This activity could be expanded so that different people consider the proposal from the viewpoint of different stakeholders.

In this chapter you will have learnt:

- the term social accounting
- how to demonstrate an awareness of non-financial factors to be considered in decision-making
- how to make critical assessments of decisions from ethical and non-financial standpoints.

AQA Examination-style questions

1   List four different stakeholders for the following businesses:
    (a)   a manufacturing international company
    (b)   a local takeaway restaurant
    (c)   a self employed gardener.

2   AQA 2007 Jun ACC4 Q4
    Explain the meaning of the term 'social accounting'.

3   Describe the financial and non-financial factors which need to be considered before investing in a new
    expensive automated factory from the viewpoint of:
    (a)   the current workforce
    (b)   the shareholders
    (c)   competitors
    (d)   the local community.

4   AQA 2004 Jun ACC7 Q4
    Millar and Williams are the sole shareholders in Milliam Ltd. Milliam Ltd trades in cosmetics made
    from ingredients not tested on animals. These ingredients are due to rise in price by 40%.

    Millar has proposed a change in supplier. The new supplier will decrease the present cost of
    ingredients by 10%, but they test their ingredients on animals. Williams is unsure as to how their
    customers will react to the proposed change in supplier, but Millar insists that they will prefer
    cheaper or static prices.

    Write a brief report to Millar and Williams considering the effect of the proposed change in supplier on
    (a)   present customers
    (b)   competitors.

5   Wenbo Zhang intends to invest £40,000 of his savings into Claxon plc, a successful UK manufacturing
    company. The directors of Claxon plc have recently discovered that the company's main supplier uses
    cheap child labour in a Third World country. This supplier has received very negative media coverage
    in the UK.
    Write a report to Wenbo Zhang as to whether he should invest his money into Claxon plc.

Glossary

A

Accounting standard: this allows financial statements to be compared over years and between companies.

Adjustment for intangible assets (goodwill): when a partner joins or leaves a partnership a change to intangible assets (goodwill) is made according to the partners' profit sharing ratios.

Adverse variance: the actual figures are worse than the standard figures in the budget, resulting in a lower actual profit than was expected.

Allocation: the process of charging costs which derive from a cost centre directly to that particular cost centre.

Analysts: their job is to closely examine trends, published accounts and the stock exchange where stocks and shares are bought and sold and make predictions.

Annual general meeting (AGM): is the yearly meeting which all the shareholders are invited to for a limited company.

Apportionment: the process of charging overhead costs to a cost centre on a rational basis.

Auditors: are independent accountants of the limited company and are responsible for the checking of the accounts to ascertain whether they provide a 'true and fair view'.

AVCO: the average cost method involves a new value of inventory (stock) being calculated each time a different cost is paid. This new cost is then used for issues until a new receipt of inventory (stock) is made.

B

Bank loans: borrowing a fixed sum over a fixed term which can be secured on assets in the business or unsecured. Interest must be paid in addition to the amount borrowed.

Bank overdrafts: represent a flexible source of finance and mean a business can spend more than they have in their bank account within a set limit.

Break-even point: this is the point at which total revenue equals total costs and so neither a profit nor a loss is made.

Budget centre: a department or area for which a budget has been set-up.

Budget: a financial plan for the future expressed in quantitative terms. It is used to control the use of resources so that the business objectives can be achieved.

Budgetary control: where responsibility to achieve the budget has been delegated to the budget centre managers.

Budgeting: the preparation of the budgets.

C

Capital deficiency: occurs when a partner has insufficient funds in their account to cover the loss of the dissolution.

Capital investment appraisal: the process of using cash flows to decide whether a capital project should be undertaken.

Cash and cash equivalents: cash held on the premises or in the bank account.

Cash flow statement: shows how cash has been generated (cash inflows) and how it has been spent (cash outflows), information not provided by the income statement or balance sheet.

Cash inflows: movements of cash into the company such as a share issue or sale of non-current assets.

Cash outflows: movements of cash out of the company, e.g. repaying loans or purchasing non-current assets.

Companies Act 1985 and 1989: these Acts govern limited companies and require that limited companies prepare and publish accounts annually. In 1989 EU directives (rules imposed by the European Union to harmonise accounting) were added.

Contribution: the money available to pay fixed costs and then once they are paid contribution becomes profit.

Cost centre: a production or service location whose costs may be attributed to cost units, e.g. a production department.

Cost driver: the factors which cause costs of an activity and also cause these costs to change.

Cost of capital: the discounting factor used in capital investment appraisals to discount future cash flows so that they are equivalent in value to cash now.

Cost pool: the location of a group of related indirect costs.

Cost unit: a unit of production or service which absorbs the cost centre's overheads costs, e.g. a product such as a television set or a service such as a restaurant meal.

Cost variance: the difference between the standard cost and the actual cost.

Current account: records all the partners' drawings, interest on drawings, interest on capital, partnership salaries and shares of residual profit or loss.

D

Debentures: loans by debenture holders who receive interest for the term of the debenture. They must not be confused with shares.

Deed of partnership: is a legal document, ideally all partnerships should have one of these so they know exactly how profits will be shared etc.

Direct cost: is identified with the cost unit. Costs attributable to a particular product, e.g. direct materials and direct labour.

Directors: are appointed by the shareholders to run the business and must produce a report as part of the published accounts.

Dissolution: takes place when a partnership ceases to continue operating. It could be because the partners want this to happen or are forced to because of problems such as lack of cash and/or profit.

Dividends: the reward to the shareholders for investing. It is not guaranteed that dividends will be paid if there is insufficient cash or profit.

F

Factory profit, or manufacturing profit: the difference between the transfer price and the production cost of completed goods, or the amount of mark-up.

Favourable variance: the actual figures are better than the standard figures in the budget resulting in a higher actual profit than was expected.

FIFO: the first in first out method involves the oldest costs being used first when inventory (stock) is issued.

Financing activities: changes in the equity capital and borrowings.

Finished goods: fully completed goods.

Fixed capital accounts: the amount of capital introduced or withdrawn by each partner is recorded in a separate account and does not alter unless agreed by the partnership.

Fixed cost: these costs do not vary with the level of production.

Flexed budget: amending standard costs for changes in levels of production.

Forecast final accounts: the forecast trading, profit and loss account and balance sheet based on the functional budgets contained within the master budget.

Full cost: the production cost of each cost unit and includes both direct and indirect costs.

G

Garner v Murray: this case set the precedent that if one partner cannot pay their share of capital deficiency then the other partners must cover the amount according to their most recent capital account ratio.

I

IAS 1 Presentation of financial statements: sets out overall requirements for the presentation of financial statements.

IAS 2 Inventories: concerned with inventory (stock) as an asset and expense and how it is valued.

IAS 7: the international standard we need to follow using the indirect method. Provides information about changes in cash and cash equivalents.

IAS 8 accounting policies, changes in accounting estimates and errors: criteria for selecting and changing accounting policies.

IAS 10 Events after reporting period: these events may affect users' interpretation of the financial statements.

IAS 16 Property, plant and equipment: concerns tangible assets held for more than one accounting period and used in the production or supply of goods and services, or for administration.

IAS 18 Revenue: includes revenue from sale of goods, rendering of services and use by others of entity assets yielding interest, royalties and dividends.

IAS 36 Impairment of assets: an asset must not be shown at more than the highest amount to be recovered through its use or sale.

IAS 37 Provisions, contingent liabilities and contingent assets: aims to ensure that appropriate measurement and recognition criteria are applied to assist users.

IAS 38 Intangible assets: non-monetary assets without physical substance.

Income statement: this replaces the trading, profit and loss account.

Indirect costs: this cost is not identified with the cost unit. Costs which cannot be attributed to a particular product, e.g. indirect labour such as the wages of supervisory staff.

Indirect method: profit or loss is adjusted to determine operating cash flow.

Intangible assets (goodwill): reflects the reputation built up by a partnership, this is an intangible asset and there are several different approaches to valuing it but it is essentially a reflection of the success of the partnership. This could be based on previous profits, e.g. it could also represent the difference between the net assets of the partnership and the amount it could be sold for.

Interest on capital: is an appropriation of the profits of the partnership and rewards those partners who have invested most.

Interest on drawings: in order to deter partners from taking excessive drawings there may be interest charged which is then debited to the partners' accounts.

Internal finance: often the first source of finance for a business to consider and involves freeing up cash within the business.

International Accounting Standard: standards set by the International Accounting Standards Board.

Inventories: stock for resale.

Investing activities: acquisition and disposal of non-current assets and investment property (investments) that are not cash equivalents.

J

JIT: just in time is an increasingly popular method of handling inventory (stock) where the minimum amount of inventory (stock) is held and replenished as required.

L

Labour budget: shows the expected amount of labour hours and the resulting cost of labour based on the production budget.

Labour efficiency variance: the difference between the actual hours used and the standard hours expected to be used, at the standard rate paid.

Labour rate variance: the difference between the actual rate paid per hour and the standard rate expected to be paid, for the actual hours used.

Labour-intensive: the production or service location has more direct labour hours than machine hours.

M

Machine-intensive: the production or service location has more direct machine hours than labour hours. The location can otherwise be known as capital-intensive.

Manufacturing account: an account prepared to calculate the production cost of manufactured goods.

Manufacturing overheads: the indirect costs incurred in the production of the products, e.g. depreciation of machinery, factory insurance and factory rent. These are often known as factory overheads.

Margin of safety: the difference between the number of sales units achieved (or maximum output) and the number of units at the break even point, where the amount of revenue (sales) achieved must exceed the break-even point otherwise a loss is made.

Marginal cost: the cost of one extra unit.

Master budget: taken from the functional budgets and consists of a budgeted income statement and forecast balance sheet.

Material price variance: the difference between the actual price paid and the standard price expected to be paid, for the actual materials used.

Material usage variance: the difference between the actual materials used and the standard materials expected to be used, at the standard price paid.

Mortgages: long-term loans specifically for purchasing property.

N

Net cash from operating activities: operating profit is adjusted for movements in receivables, inventories etc. to obtain this figure.

Net present value: a capital investment appraisal method which uses the present value of net cash flows to ascertain whether the capital project should be undertaken on financial grounds.

Non-current (Fixed) assets: the term used for fixed assets which are expensive items bought not primarily to resell but to help generate profits.

Non-current liabilities: what the company owes and is due to be repaid after 12 months such as a loan.

O

Operating activities: revenue-producing activities that are not investing or financing.

Ordinary shares: these are the most common type of share issued. An ordinary shareholder receives a variable dividend based on profit in return for their investment.

Over-absorption: occurs when more units are produced than was predicted in the budget and therefore more overheads are absorbed into the cost unit.

Overhead absorption rate (OAR): the rate which is used to absorb the overheads into the cost unit. It is calculated as either rate per direct machine hour or rate per direct labour hour depending on which the department uses the most.

P

Partnership Act 1890: this states, for example how to share profits or losses if no agreement is in place.

Partnership salary: a payment to a partner and appears in the appropriation section, not with expenses. It also is entered in the partner's current account. It may reflect that some partners may

contribute more working hours than others.

Payables (creditors) budget: a summary of the expected movement in money owed by the business to the suppliers.

Payback: a calculation of how long it takes to generate enough cash inflows to cover the initial cost of a capital project.

Periodic method: inventory (stock) is valued at the end of a financial period. It is the quickest method and should always be used when calculating the FIFO method even when perpetual is asked for as the same answer is found.

Perpetual method: a running balance is kept using this method and a new value of inventory (stock) calculated each time inventory (stock) is received or issued.

Potential investors: are people who may wish to buy shares in a company. The element of risk and potential reward is important to this group and also whether they intend to invest for the short or long term.

Preference shares: are a lower risk option to ordinary shares but as a consequence offer a lower return.

Prime costs: the total of all direct costs incurred when producing the products.

Production budget: the calculation of expected production in units based on the information from the revenue (sales) budget and accounting for movements in inventory (stock) of finished goods.

Production cost of manufactured goods (also known as 'cost of production' or 'production cost of completed goods'): is the total of all the costs of manufacturing the products.

Production department: where the product is actually made, e.g. the machining department.

Profit and loss appropriation account: this account records the distribution of profits among partners based on any agreement made by the partners. Where there is no agreement the terms of the Partnership Act 1890 should be applied. The account includes interest on drawings, interest on capital, partnership salaries and the share of the residual profit or loss.

Purchases budget: a calculation of the expected value of purchases of materials based on the production levels as shown by the production budget.

R

Realisation account: used to close the partnership and calculate the profit or loss for the partners once all the assets have been sold or taken over.

Receivables: money owed by debtors.

Receivables budget: a summary of the expected movement in money owed by the customers to the business.

Retirement of a partner: a structural change to the partnership and creates a 'new' partnership as a result. When a partner decides to retire we need to calculate the latest profit, the current worth of the partnership and perhaps reward the retiring partner for goodwill built up.

Revaluation account: fixed assets such as premises will have normally increased in value but others may have decreased such as inventory (stock). This account records the changes in value.

Revenue (sales) budget: a summary of the expected revenue (sales) units and revenue (sales) value for the future.

Revenue (sales) price variance: the difference between the actual selling price per product and the standard selling price expected per product, for the actual units sold.

Revenue (sales) volume variance: the difference between the actual number of units sold and the standard number of units expected to be sold, at the standard selling price.

Revenue variance: the difference between the standard revenue and actual revenue.

Risk: all lenders have to decide on the level of risk a business

presents. This is based on past experience, future predictions and on the current state of the business. The lender must decide how likely they are to be repaid and whether the likely return is worth the potential risk figures such as profit, loss, opening or closing capital.

Royalties: a sum of money paid to the inventor of a product for the right of use of his ideas.

S

Sale or return: goods are supplied and do not need to be paid for until they are sold and can be returned to the supplier if they don't sell.

Schedule of non-current assets: records the movement of non-current assets and the depreciation attached to the movements.

Semi-variable costs: are partly fixed and partly variable.

Service department: these departments support the other departments, e.g. technical support and canteen.

Social accounting: this term is applied when businesses are accountable to society at large, whereby they must consider both the non-financial and financial aspects of every decision they make.

Stakeholders: any group or individual who has an interest in the activities of the business.

Standard cost card: specifies the standard costs predetermined for one unit.

Standard cost: a predetermined cost which should be achieved through an efficient working environment.

Standard costing: the preparation and use of standard costs, including the calculation of variances.

Statement of affairs: a basic balance sheet which can be used to calculate missing in the role of the borrower, the business also has to weigh up the risks of any source of finance. The business must consider its

financial needs, as well as the complications associates with each source.

Statement of changes in capital (equity): records the issue of shares.

Sub-variance: each total variance can be broken down into two sub-variances that analyse the reasons for the variance in more detail.

T

Time value of money: this concept states that money received or paid out in the future does not have the same value as money today.

Trade and other receivables: includes trade receivables (debtors) and prepayments, amounts owed to us or that we have paid ahead for, e.g. rent and insurance.

Trade payables: what the company owes to trade creditors.

Trade receivables (creditors) budget: a summary of the expected movement in money owed by the business to the suppliers.

Trade receivables (debtors) budget: a summary of the expected movement in money owed by the customers to the business.

Transfer price: production cost of completed goods plus a percentage mark-up.

U

Under-absorption: this occurs when fewer units are produced than was predicted in the budget and therefore not all the overheads are absorbed into the cost unit.

Unrealised profit on finished goods: this is profit which is not recognised until the stock is sold and a contract of sale has been negotiated.

V

Variable cost: these costs vary with the level of production.

Variance: the difference between a standard cost or revenue and an actual cost or revenue.

W

Work in progress: partly finished goods.

Index

Note: Key terms and the page on which they appear in the key term box are in **bold**